General Facts Everyone Assumes You Know

▼ If you see C> or C:\> on-screen when you start the computer, your computer is se

▼ If you see Program Manager on-screen, your computer is set up to run Microsoft W

▼ To start Windows (if it doesn't start automatically), type **WIN** at the DOS prompt

Off and Running with DOS

▼ To start a program, type the program's name and press Enter.

▼ If you make a mistake while typing, use the Backspace key to correct the mistake.

Off and Running with Windows

To start a program, click on the Window menu and click on the program's group window name. (Try Applications.) When the program icons appear, double-click on the icon of the program you want to start.

Key Into This

In DOS Programs:

Key or Key Combo	What the Key or Combo Does
Enter	Sends a command to the computer
Ctrl+C or Ctrl+Break	Cancels a DOS command
Ctrl+S or Pause	Pauses a long directory list
Ctrl+Alt+Del	Resets the computer (wipes out memory!)
Prt Scrn	Prints whatever is on-screen

In DOS and Windows Programs:

Key or Key Combo	What the Key or Combo Does
Backspace	Rubs out the character left of the cursor
Enter	Confirms the command and continues
Caps Lock	Turns on and off capital letters
Num Lock	Toggles the keys on the numeric keypad between numbers and cursor movement
→	Moves the cursor right
←	Moves the cursor left
↓	Moves the cursor down
↑	Moves the cursor up
PgDn	Scrolls down one screen
PgUp	Scrolls up one screen
Home	Moves the cursor to the beginning of the line
End	Moves the cursor to the end of the line
Esc	Cancels a command
F1	Gets help

In Windows and Windows Programs:

Key or Key Combo	What the Key or Combo Does
Alt+underlined letter	Opens a menu
Underlined letter	Chooses a menu option from a menu
Alt+Esc	Cycles through open programs
Alt+Tab	Displays open program names in an on-screen box. Hold down Alt and keep pressing Tab until the program you want is displayed; then release both keys.
Ctrl+Esc	Displays the task list
Alt, space bar, N	Minimizes an application window
Alt, space bar, X	Maximizes an application window
Ctrl+F4	Closes an application window
Alt+Backspace	Undoes the last editing change
Alt+F4	Exits the program
F1	Gets help

What's in a Name?

▼ DOS and Windows file names have two parts, the file name (up to 8 characters long) and the extension (up to 3 characters long). The two are separated by a period, as in JUNK.DOC or TRASH.WK1. The extension is optional.

▼ File names can't contain spaces. They also can't contain any of these characters:

. " / \ [ ] : * | < > + = ; , ?

Drive Yourself Nuts

▼ Most computers have at least one floppy disk drive and one hard disk drive.

▼ The hard disk is called drive C.

▼ The first floppy is called drive A.

▼ If you have two floppy drives, the second is drive B.

▼ Your system might have additional drives.

Directory Assistance

▼ The root directory symbol is a backslash (\ ). C:\ indicates the root directory of drive C.

▼ The root directory of drive C probably contains one or more subdirectories. *Subdirectories* have names preceded by a backslash, like \DOCS. A subdirectory can, in turn, have its own subdirectories. In \DOCS\HATEMAIL, \HATEMAIL is a subdirectory of \DOCS.

▼ A *path name* is a file name that includes the file's subdirectory location (as in \DOCS\HATEMAIL\JUNK.DOC). Note that you have to put a backslash before the file's name (\JUNK.DOC).

▼ A *filespec* tells all about a file's location, including disk and name (as in C:\DOCS\HATEMAIL\JUNK.DOC).

Go Wild

▼ The ? wild card matches any single character.

▼ The * wild card matches any character(s).

▼ *.* (star-dot-star) matches all file names.

I HATE

PCs

Bryan Pfaffenberger

I Hate PCs

Copyright © 1993 by Que® Corporation

Library of Congress Catalog No.: 93-83858

ISBN: 1-56529-254-5

95 94 93   6 5 4 3 2

Interpretation of the printing code: the rightmost double-digit number is the year of the book's printing; the rightmost single-digit number, the number of the book's printing. For example, a printing code of 93-1 shows that the first printing of the book occurred in 1993.

Screen reproductions in this book were created using Collage Plus from Inner Media, Inc., Hollis, NH.

Cover illustration by Jeff MacNelly.

Publisher: David P. Ewing

Associate Publisher: Rick Ranucci

Publishing Plan Manager: Thomas H. Bennett

Operations Manager: Sheila Cunningham

About the Author

Bryan Pfaffenberger, called "Hamburger," "Cheeseburger," and other injurious things during painful years at school, at last found obscurity as a sincere, mild-mannered, and bumbling professor at a small Midwestern liberal arts college. But this peaceful existence was rudely interrupted after his 1981 purchase of a Kaypro computer, which occasioned a new round of ridicule. After spending a few months learning how to format a disk, Bryan declared to his astonished friends, family, and colleagues, "If I can figure this out, anyone can."

Since then, Bryan has written more than 35 books that translate computer mumbo-jumbo into plain English. An example: his best-selling *Que's Computer User's Dictionary*, with more than 250,000 copies in print.

Bryan knows that computers can help people work better, smarter, and faster, but they can also be a pain in the you-know-what. Worse, most computer books throw all the facts at you, as if you had to know everything. Isn't that sick?

Que's *I Hate...* books reflect Bryan's philosophy: "Computer books should teach only what you need to know. They should tell you what parts of the program are pointless and forgettable. And they shouldn't ask you to plow through 200 pages of tutorials just so that you can learn how to print a document."

Bryan's writing style gets right to the point, with an informal and humorous approach. With *I Hate PCs* as your guide, you may not wind up loving your computer—but you'll know how to fake it.

I HATE PCs!

Credits

Title Manager:
Shelley O'Hara

Production Editor:
Cindy Morrow

Technical Editor:
Lynda Fox

Book Designer:
Scott Cook

Novice Reviewer:
Gary Keegan

Editorial Assistants:
Julia Blount
Sandra Naito

Production Team:
Claudia Bell
Julie Brown
Jodie Cantwell
Paula Carroll
Laurie Casey
Brook Farling
Audra Gable
Carla Hall-Batton
Heather Kaufman
Caroline Roop
Linda Seifert
Johnna VanHoose

Composed in *Goudy* and *MCPdigital* by Que Corporation.

I HATE PCs!

Acknowledgments

A lot of people contributed to this book, in so many ways. But I'd like to begin by thanking the department store employee who, while trying to demonstrate how to start a computer, picked up the mouse and attempted to turn on the computer by using it like a TV remote control. It was then that I realized that millions of people would probably appreciate having all "The Basic Stuff About PCs" explained to them in ways that aren't socially embarrassing.

My title manager, Shelley O'Hara, just happens to be the best in the business, and contributed to this book in zillions of ways—thanks, Shelley. To Rick Ranucci go my thanks for inspiration, guidance, and encouragement. I'd also like to thank my agent, Bill Gladstone, for handling the business stuff so that I could sit around and think up Top Ten lists unperturbed by things like the movie rights to this book (any action there yet, Bill?). Thanks are due, too, to Cindy Morrow, for the usual top-notch Que editorial job, to Scott Cook for the design, to Jeff MacNelly for the cool cartoons, and to everyone at Que who has worked so hard to bring this book to fruition.

Trademark Acknowledgments

All terms mentioned in this book that are known to be trademarks or service marks have been appropriately capitalized. Que cannot attest to the accuracy of this information. Use of a term in this book should not be regarded as affecting the validity of any trademark or service mark.

1-2-3 and Lotus are registered trademarks of Lotus Development Corporation.

DOS, Microsoft Excel, Microsoft Windows, and Microsoft Word are registered trademarks of Microsoft Corporation.

IBM is a registered trademark of International Business Machines, Inc.

WordPerfect is a registered trademark of WordPerfect Corporation.

I HATE PCs!

Contents at a Glance

Table of Contents

I HATE PCs!

V Quick & Dirty Dozens ⠀⠀⠀⠀⠀⠀⠀⠀⠀⠀⠀⠀⠀⠀⠀**325**

Quick 'n Dirty Dozens ⠀⠀⠀⠀⠀⠀⠀⠀⠀⠀⠀⠀⠀⠀⠀**327**

Index ⠀⠀⠀⠀⠀⠀⠀⠀⠀⠀⠀⠀⠀⠀⠀**355**

I HATE PCs

Introduction

If you hate PCs, but you have to use one, you've come to the right place. This book begins with a simple, dangerous, and irreverent premise: You don't need to be "improved" by spending months learning and memorizing every last thing about the PC. PCs are just tools you can use. If there's something you need to know, you can just look it up. And that's true whether you're using DOS or Windows. (If you don't know what these words mean, don't worry—you will.)

This book provides an easy, fun introduction to PCs. What's a PC? Any IBM or IBM-compatible personal computer.

This book isn't like other computer books, which are written with a secret (but ill-disguised) desire to foist Computer Literacy upon an unsuspecting book-buying public. *I Hate PCs* doesn't try to turn you into a computer-loving vegetable. It includes just enough information about PCs to help you get going, produce good work, and get on with the rest of your life (which is already in progress).

Some Assumptions about You

Let's be frank. You're reading this because you're thinking, "I've got to get some computer skills." But inside, you were thinking, "Is there any way I can get out of this?"

If so, welcome to a club recently joined by millions. Like it or not, you have a PC. Or you've been stuck with one at work. Someone has already set it up for you, and turned you loose after hitting you with a few unintelligible do's and don'ts. Maybe you've cracked open a few computer books or manuals, only to find hundreds of pages of incomprehensible junk that left you even *more* confused.

The computer—and all those horrible computer manuals—don't seem to understand that you have a *life*. You have more important things to do than spend the next six months taking computer lessons. You're definitely not in love with PCs. You don't even find them attractive. You don't want to have to "learn" stuff, chapter-by-chapter, in a process that goes on for weeks. You don't want to have to memorize anything.

If this picture describes you, congratulations—you're normal, and you've a great chance of succeeding with the computer. Everyone who uses computers is not enthralled with them—any more than everyone who pounds a nail is enthralled with hammers. These people don't spend time fussing over every last little thing for hours and hours. They just do their work, efficiently and competently, and then shut the thing down.

If you can relate to this intro, *I Hate PCs* is the perfect book for you. This book covers everything you do with the PC on a day-to-day basis, and does so in a handy, look-it-up-when-you-need-it format. What it *doesn't* cover is all the rest of the useless, technical mummery that nerds like myself think everyone should adore.

About This Book's Icons

Flip through the book. Do you notice those pictures in the margins? These pictures—called *icons*—signal you to the type of information contained next to the icon. If you're not interested in this type of information, skip it. Here's what the icons mean:

"I HATE THIS!"

This icon tells you when the computer is about to pull a fast one on you. By reading the text next to this icon, you can sidestep—or at least remedy—some of the PC's quirks.

TIP

This icon alerts you to shortcuts, tricks, and time-savers.

EXPERTS ONLY

This icon flags skippable technical stuff that I couldn't resist including. I am, after all, a nerd, although I now understand, after a painful process of self-examination, that most of the rest of the world does not share my enthusiasm for technology.

CAUTION

Warning! Danger! This icon warns you about those pitfalls and traps to avoid.

BUZZWORDS

This icon warns you that you're about to learn technospeak—some nifty word or phrase like *byte* or *bit* or *blip* or *blurp*.

PART I

Getting Acquainted

Includes:

CHAPTER 1

Stuff People Think You Already Know

IN A NUTSHELL

▼ Why there's such a fuss over computers

▼ Why there's a distinction between software and hardware

▼ How to recognize the various parts of a computer system

▼ What an "operating system" is and why it's needed

▼ What Windows is and why it's cool

I HATE PCs!

There are more than 100 million personal computers now in existence worldwide. For many people, that's 100 million reasons for panic. Anxieties about computers vary from person to person, but perhaps you'll recognize yourself in one of these utterings:

▼ "I'm afraid I'll ruin something."

▼ "I'm afraid I won't know what to do."

▼ "I'm afraid everyone will laugh at me when I press the wrong key."

▼ "I'm afraid I'm going to have to read those big, thick computer books and memorize everything."

▼ "I'm afraid my 12-year-old kid knows more than I do."

Lots of computers, lots of people, lots of fears. But, if you've picked up this book, chances are you've decided to do something about those fears. Or maybe you've been given no choice—your company, in its infinite wisdom, has plunked a PC on your desk. For whatever reason, you're about to have a Close Encounter of the Third Kind with a computer, and you aren't happy about it.

What's really so scary about computers? For most people, it's the feeling that you're at the absolute beginning of a three-year program of grueling, post-graduate study, during which your shortcomings—like rusty math or poor memorization skills—will become all too evident. No wonder you feel like fleeing in the opposite direction—and fast. If so, read on, read on.

The truth about computers

▼ There's hardly anything about computers that's worth learning, memorizing, and regurgitating in the classic grade-school sense. "Computer Literacy" is a crock.

I HATE PCs!

▼ The only stuff you need to learn about computers is what you need to know to get your work done.

▼ You don't need to memorize anything. It's far better just to look up the information you need, when you need it.

▼ Remember the 20/80 rule: Only about 20 percent of the information about computers is really useful. Put the useful 20 percent to work and forget the other 80 percent. You can always get help from your neighborhood computer nerd if you ever need anything from the 80-percent category.

▼ The basic 20 percent is pretty easy—anybody can do it. *You* can do it. You're already doing stuff that's harder than this—like driving a car or figuring out the *Jeopardy!* challenge.

▼ This book's organization reflects the 20/80 rule: The first four chapters are a "mini-book" that contain the most useful information. If you read only these chapters, you'll know enough to get started with computing! You can read the rest of the chapters as you please or as the need arises.

"I HATE THIS!"

Compute? What do you mean? I have to take algebra again?

Lay that math anxiety aside. "Computer" is a very inaccurate name. Sure, computers can process numbers, but they can also work with words, pictures, music—any kind of information. The French, who like to assign their own names to things, don't use the word "computer." They call computers "information processors" instead. I hate to admit it, but they've got a point.

I HATE PCs!

Let's Start at the Very Beginning

Don't be embarrassed about starting at the *do-re-mi* level. You're not alone. Consider the following true story about a salesperson at a department store. When asked to turn on a computer for a demonstration, he pointed the little mouse thing at the screen and tried to start the computer by clicking the mouse button (as if the mouse were a TV remote control). Of course, this was witnessed with delight by a crowd of snickering, 9-year-old computer jockeys. Well, at least we know enough to brush our teeth in the morning without being reminded ten times.

So: The beginning. What *are* computers, anyway? And why have people gone out and bought so many of them?

HUH?
BUZZWORDS

COMPUTER

An incredibly *flexible* piece of electronic junk that can be modified to do a boatload of very diverse tasks. Write a letter. Calculate a budget. Play a game. Compose a rock opera. And the bright spot about computers is that you don't have to change the actual physical aspects of the computer in order to get it to do different things. You just put in a different program. This is a lot cheaper and more convenient than having to rewire the electronics inside the box.

HUH?
BUZZWORDS

PROGRAM

A list of instructions that tell the computer what to do. People who write programs are called *programmers*. Happily, you don't have to be a programmer to use the computer. You can buy and use programs that are already written. These programs can do lots of different tasks. And, they're getting easier to use. When you've learned how to use your programs, you've learned enough—you can leave the more complicated stuff to technoweenies.

Computers are popular because they're so flexible. You can do lots of different things without having to buy lots of different machines. Of course, many people use a computer just because it does one thing very well. For me, that one thing is word processing. I wrote my first book using a typewriter—and frankly, there wouldn't have been a Book Number 2 if I had to repeat all that typing, retyping, and manual cutting-and-pasting. With word processing software, I can easily revise my manuscript so that it's perfect *before* I print it. But I also use my computer for other stuff, too—like tracking business expenses, sending faxes hither and yon, making transparencies for presentations, and piloting my simulated Cessna 172 underneath the Golden Gate Bridge.

There are lots of different kinds of computers. You've probably heard of *mainframe computers*, those huge behemoths that big companies use to crank out payroll checks, bills, and the like. This book is about *personal computers*. Personal computers, unlike their larger cousins, are designed to meet an *individual's* computing needs. The term *PC*, incidentally, has become more or less synonymous with IBM and IBM-compatible personal computers, the subject of this book. There are other types of personal computers, such as Apple's Macintosh, but that's another book entirely. This book is for anyone using an IBM personal computer, or an IBM *clone* or *compatible*.

BUZZWORDS

CLONE or COMPATIBLE

The first IBM personal computers were made by—you guessed it—IBM. But soon copies appeared. The copies are called *clones* or *compatibles*. There's nothing wrong with using a clone. Clones can be great machines. And, they're perfectly legit, so don't worry about the FBI showing up and dragging you off kicking and screaming. The real cheap clones have thin, tinny cabinets and mushy, spongy keyboards, but frankly, the electronic stuff inside is just about the same no matter which brand you buy.

Ware, Hard and Soft

(It takes two)

You already understand this distinction. But, technical people just *love* to make up new words for things. Part of the tedium of learning computers is learning how to speak a few words of computerese.

BUZZWORDS

HARDWARE

The physical parts of the computer, like the printer. Or the mouse. Or the disk drive.

BUZZWORDS

SOFTWARE

Collectively, the programs that give computer hardware the ability to do something more interesting than just sit there and take up space on the desk.

What's All This Junk on My Desk?

The following picture shows the hardware parts that you see in the usual, garden-variety computer system. The *system* part implies that all the components have been selected because they work together harmoniously. (The television thing, for example, has to be matched to something inside.)

I HATE PCs!

System unit

Neighborhood
computer nerd

Monitor

Printer

Keyboard

Mouse

CHAPTER 1

Hardware Part	The Scoop
System Unit	This is the cabinet that houses the computer's electronic inside parts. On the front, you see one or two slot-like openings for those computer disk things. Coming out of the back are just tons of cables. The power switch is located on the right side, probably, although some computers put the switch on the back panel so that no one can find it. Chapter 5 goes into the stuff that's inside this cabinet, but it's not for the faint of heart.
Hard Disk	You can't see this part because it's inside the system unit; but you can hear it humming once the computer gets going. It also has its own little light on the system unit's front panel. This light tells you when the hard disk is working (instead of just spinning idly). The hard disk is a computer disk like the ones you stick into the slot, *except* that it has a super-huge capacity and spins at a blazing rate inside its own, hermetically sealed case. You store your programs and your work on the hard disk. Hard disks (as well as the other kind) are covered in Chapter 7.
Keyboard	The computer keyboard lets you do two things: give commands to the computer, and do your work. There are lots of funny keys (like Ctrl and Alt) that you don't find on a typewriter; these do specific, computery things and are discussed in Chapter 8.

I HATE PCs!

"I HATE THIS!"

Do I have to know how to *type* to use this thing?

Not necessarily. If you're planning to do lots of writing, learning how to type would be wise. But if you're doing stuff like balancing your checkbook, figuring out loan balances, maintaining a mailing list, or just playing some of those cool computer games, typing skills really aren't necessary. And, if you like, the computer can teach you to type. Get yourself a copy of Que's Typing Tutor, a computerized typing teacher that gives you great lessons and monitors your progress just like a human typing teacher would.

Hardware Part	The Scoop
Monitor	This resembles a television, but instead of seeing Oprah, you see your work. It has its own power switch, as well as brightness and contrast knobs. Monitors are the subject of Chapter 9.
Mouse	A little box the size of a bar of soap. When you move this thing, it spins a little ball on the bottom of the mouse, causing a pointer to move on-screen. With some applications, you can do things by pointing the mouse pointer to them and clicking the mouse button. Some people really like this capability and other people hate it (especially touch typists who dislike taking their fingers away from the keyboard).

continues

I HATE PCs!

Hardware Part	The Scoop
Printer	This probably looks like a little photo-copying machine without the glass part, although there's a lot of diversity—there are zillions of different printers available for PCs. The computer sends your document to the printer, which prints it. Chapter 10 surveys the often confusing world of printers.
Neighborhood Nerd	By far the most important part of your system, needed for many things like getting the system set up to run and dealing with certain problems that beginners can't handle. Your company might actually pay such an individual to wander around and be helpful.

"I HATE THIS!"

I've gained 15 pounds since I started using my computer!

When you use the computer, you just sit, sit, sit. And to keep up with all the verbiage going by on-screen, you might be tempted to munch, munch, munch. All those potato-chip carbohydrates produce a "high" that seems to help when you're trying to figure out what to do next. But, let's be honest, it isn't too healthy. You can get the same "high" from taking exercise breaks every couple of hours. Try it!

The Operating System

(Your OS is DOS)

You put different programs into your computer to do different things that are useful to you. But there's a type of program your computer needs so that it can function. This is called the *operating system* (abbreviated OS). Basically, an operating system is a computer program that helps the computer system's parts work together in a useful way.

The operating system for IBM and IBM-compatible personal computers is called MS-DOS. Most people just shorten this to "DOS," which rhymes with "boss."

Much of the stuff that DOS does you'll never be aware of, because it goes on automatically. The part you're aware of has to do with various system maintenance procedures, such as preparing those funny little disks for use or erasing information you don't need.

Getting a fix on DOS

▼ Your computer needs MS-DOS to run. One of the first things that happens when you turn on your computer is that it starts MS-DOS. See Chapter 2 for more information on starting your system.

▼ The "MS" part of MS-DOS stands for Microsoft (of Microsoft Corporation fame), the company that publishes DOS (and has gotten pretty rich doing it).

▼ DOS can be pretty complicated, but you only need to learn a little to use the computer effectively. Ignore the rest.

▼ You find more information about DOS in Chapter 3 and Chapter 15. This information is enough to get you going with your PC. If you'd like more information on DOS, see this book's companion volume, *I Hate DOS* (also written by Yours Truly).

Does Your Computer Do Windows?

Your computer might be set up to run Microsoft Windows after you turn it on. If so, you'll know it, because you'll see something called "Program Manager" on-screen. (If your computer isn't set up to run Windows, you see something like this: `C:\>`.)

Unlike DOS, Microsoft Windows is optional. It isn't *necessary* that you have Microsoft Windows in order for the computer to run. Basically, it just makes your computer easier and more fun to use. It also enhances the computer's capabilities. There's a pretty good chance that your computer is set up to run Windows when you turn it on.

Picture yourself in a world full of Windows...

▼ If you see something called "Program Manager" when you turn on your computer, Chapter 4 will help you get going. You can skip Chapter 3 if you want.

▼ When your computer is running Windows, DOS is still running in the background, behind the scenes. You can even switch back to DOS, if you want. But most people don't want to. For them, one of the best things about Windows is that they can forget about DOS.

▼ Windows is at its best with *Windows applications*. A Windows application is a program that requires Windows, and is specifically designed to take advantage of the cool, easy-to-use features of Windows.

▼ You can use a Windows accessory called File Manager to take care of those pesky system maintenance tasks, such as copying your work or formatting disks. Chapter 16 covers the use of Windows for such tasks.

▼ Chapters 4 and 16 of this book cover enough Windows knowledge to get you going with your PC. If you'd like more information on Windows, see the companion volume to this book: *I Hate Windows*.

▼ A program that doesn't require Windows, but does require DOS, is called a *DOS application*. When programs are described in ads, the copy usually reads "For DOS" or "For Windows" so that you can tell the difference. Many programs are available in two versions: one for DOS and one for Windows.

▼ Windows has one big shortcoming: You need a pretty zippy, up-to-date computer system to run Windows. Chapter 5 has more information on the general subject of computer zippiness, in case you're interested.

Where Do I Go from Here?

It's time to turn on the computer, and see what comes up. Chapter 2 goes into the basics of starting your system and deciphering what you see. If your computer is set up to run DOS, you'll see the notorious C:\> prompt; turn to Chapter 3 for counseling, solace, and guidance. If your computer is set up to run Microsoft Windows, count your blessings, and turn to Chapter 4. Or, just leave the darned thing turned off and go do something fun.

CHAPTER 1

Top Ten Uses for an Unplugged Computer

10. Large, flat surface of system unit ideal for stacking correspondence that you really do plan to answer some day

9. Use Post-It notes to affix various reminders and to-do lists to screen

8. Use floppy disk drive to stash wafer-thin chocolate snack when fellow dieters stop by to chat

7. Rub keyboard over neck, back for relaxing, Dozens-O-Fingers massage

6. Hang mouse from doorknob to make hilarious cat toy

5. Use 12-foot printer cable to practice lasso techniques

4. Printer paper tray provides secure, yet accessible, storage for current issue of *Soap Opera Digest*

3. Bulky system components are easily arranged so that entire desktop is covered, leaving no room for additional work

2. Stack system unit, monitor, computer manuals so that Philodendron, African violet have sufficient light from window

1. Position computer so that boss cannot see you reading romance, science fiction novels

CHAPTER 2

On My Mark, Engage
(Starting Your System)

IN A NUTSHELL

- ▼ What's contained on the computer's front panel
- ▼ How to find the power switch and turn on the computer
- ▼ What to do if the system doesn't start
- ▼ What goes by on-screen after you start the computer
- ▼ What to do after the computer finishes its startup ordeal

omputers can be vexing things to get started—it's tough to find the switches. Worse, the computer won't start if there's a disk in the disk drive, and thousands of incomprehensible things happen on-screen for a while until the darned thing settles down. This chapter examines the computer startup procedure, reassures you about things that would otherwise scare you to death, and helps you avoid those little pitfalls that computers like to throw in your way. You also learn what to do if something really does go seriously wrong, which happens every once in a while.

Front Panel Stuff

Some computers have switches, buttons, indicators, and small Garfield dolls on the front panel. You can ignore most of this stuff, but here's a quick rundown of the things that might be useful.

Item	The Scoop
Key	Some computers come with a roundish looking keyhole that lets you lock the computer (with a roundish-looking key). That funny diagram is supposed to be a lock, get it? If it's open, the computer is unlocked and you can start it. If it's closed, the computer is locked, and you can't start it.

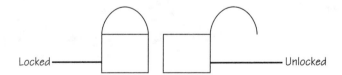

Locked ———   ——— Unlocked

"I HATE THIS!"

Where's the darned key?

If the computer is locked and you can't find the key, here's a tip: a lot of clone manufacturers attach those little round keys to the exhaust fan grill on the back of the computer. Take a look. Otherwise, find the box the computer came in and look underneath all those big pieces of Styrofoam.

These keys are really only intended to deter amateurs; they aren't to lock out users. If you can't find the key, try using a coworker's little round key; chances are, it will unlock your computer.

Item	The Scoop
Reset Button	You push this button to *reboot* your computer. Rebooting (restarting) is necessary after a computer crash (yes, they happen). Chapter 19 fills you in on the unpleasant topic of computer crashes.

CAUTION

Don't hit the Reset button while you're working with the computer. This not only restarts the computer; it also clears the computer's memory—and gets rid of all your unsaved work. Reset your computer only after you're certain your computer has crashed. Chapter 19 offers specific guidance, but for now, remember that the computer might not have crashed; you might have gotten into some part of the program that just works differently. Explore all possible alternatives before rebooting your system.

continues

I HATE PCs!

Item	The Scoop
Turbo Switch	Your computer may not have this, but if it does, leave it on. Some computers have two speeds, Regular and Turbo (super). When the Turbo switch is engaged, you get super speed. (When the little light is on, your computer's running at super speed instead of regular speed.)

EXPERTS ONLY

I can't drive 55!

Back in the old days, some programs actually *required* a slow computer, and they'd act funny (or crash) if you used the Turbo speed. The Turbo button is included so that if you're using one of these programs, you can turn off Turbo speed. But I can't think of any current programs that require a slower speed—quite the opposite, in fact. Most of today's programs are so big, fat, and feature-packed that they run at a decidedly sluggish pace on most systems, leaving users fantasizing about ever-more-speedy machines. Leave the Turbo switch engaged. (The switch is engaged when the Turbo light is on.)

Power Light	This little light essentially just shows you that the computer is turned on.
Disk Activity Lights	These little lights come on when the disks are doing something important, like saving your work. The hard disk's activity light is probably somewhere on the front panel. This light doesn't really give you any useful information except that the drive's alive and kicking, which is sometimes reassuring to know. The activity lights for the floppy

Item	The Scoop
	disk drives, the ones with the slots, are right on the front panel of the drive. These lights (unlike the hard disk's activity light) have some practical value—you shouldn't remove a disk while a floppy disk drive's activity light is on or you might scramble and poach the data on the disk.

CAUTION

> When the activity light is on, leave the disk in the drive. If you try to remove it, the disk drive might "smear" data across the disk surface, totally wrecking the data stored on it. Wait for the light to go off, and then take out the disk.

Turning on the Computer

(Why they hide the switch)

The big moment is here: it's you and the PC. You're ready to rev her up.

First, make sure there's no disk in drive A. Your computer won't start correctly if there's a disk in drive A, which is usually the top one if you have two drives. If drive A has a latch that covers the drive door, you can remove the disk by flipping the latch up so the disk pops out. If drive A doesn't have a latch but does have a little button, just push the button; the disk pops out.

Now that this disk drive thing is settled, the next question is: where's the switch?

If you're lucky, your system is hooked up to a *power strip*—an electrical strip with several outlets. (You have to buy the power strip; it doesn't come with the computer.) If so, it's pretty easy to turn on the system: just flip the switch on the power strip. This one switch probably turns on everything—the CPU, monitor, printer, and so on.

If there's no power strip, you have to hunt down the switches for each component. Start with the computer (the box thing) and monitor (the TV thing).

Look for a button on the front of the computer, or failing that, a big red switch on the right side of the computer. But be forewarned: some system designers place the switch on the back panel where (1) you fear you'll be electrocuted if you stick your finger in the wrong hole and (2) you may jar loose some of the data cables, resulting in (even more) bizarre system behavior. As you tenderly but blindly explore the back panel looking for the switch, be careful to avoid the cables, power cords, and the large, poisonous bugs and snakes that creep back there seeking warmth and darkness.

Monitor switches are even harder to find. Look on the front, back, right side, left side, bottom, and top of the monitor. After that, kick it.

Checklist

▼ If you found both switches, you'll know it. The computer hums, buzzes, clicks, and whirs. These are happy noises. A great deal of information also flashes past on the screen, much faster than you can read it. Ignore it—or if you insist, read the next section, "What You See."

▼ If nothing happens, make sure that all the stuff is plugged in. If it *still* won't start, make sure that there's power going to the plugs where the computer stuff is plugged in; plug in a little desk lamp and try turning it on. If it won't work, call an electrician.

Turning on a computer is called *booting the computer* by technoweenies.

BOOT
To start the computer fresh, with a clear memory. Technoweenies like to distinguish between a *cold boot* (you turn the system on after it has been off for a while) and a *warm boot* (you restart the system after it has been on, for example, by pressing the Reset button).

What You See

(But may not get)

When your computer starts, many things happen—probably too quickly to see and definitely acceptable to ignore. Here's a handy guide, in case you're curious about what's going on. If you're not curious, skip this entire section.

The BIOS Message

BIOS message. The very first thing to appear on-screen is the BIOS message. You see something like this:

```
Turbo 386 Chipset ROM BIOS Version 8.91
(c)1992 Technology Enterprises, Ltd.
```

I HATE PCs!

TIP

If you hear something but nothing appears on-screen, make sure that you turned on the monitor. Also, check the brightness and contrast control; somebody may have turned the brightness all the way off.

BIOS is short for *basic input-output system*. It's a mini-program that's loaded into your computer at the start of every operating session. This program comes from a little chip called ROM (short for *read-only memory*). This ROM chip contains a permanently encoded program. What's BIOS for? When you turn on your computer, its memory is cleared. Blank. Zilch. Nada. Zero. It can't remember its own name. It can't remember what town it's in. It can't even find its fingers and toes. BIOS tells it very basic stuff like,

You are a computer. Your first task is to look for DOS.

And that, as you will see, is just what it does.

TIP

If your computer is acting so strange that even Chapter 19 can't help, a call to the computer manufacturer's technical support hotline may be in order. They're sure to ask, "Which BIOS version do you have?" With most "clones," you can answer this question just by restarting the computer and looking at this first stuff that appears.

Say "Aaahh," and Let's Check Those Memory Chips

The next on-screen event is the *memory check*. Your computer might scramble your data if the memory isn't working perfectly, so your computer runs this check every time you switch on the power (*reboot*). If the

numbers zoom up to a certain figure and then stop, and the computer keeps going, the memory check has been successful. (Displaying a message like `Your memory is fine` would be too simple.)

"I HATE THIS!"

> ## "What the &%$# is a parity error?"
> If the memory check finds a mistake, you may see a message such as Parity error or Memory error; then the system shuts down. Obviously, this is bad news, but don't panic—one of those little memory chips is bad, and fixing it is not going to be too expensive. Look at the screen; you probably see a code that combines letters and numbers in a weird way. Write it down. This will help the computer repair technician to find and replace the errant memory chip. Then turn off your computer, and it's off to the repair shop.

Hello, Drive A?

The next startup event is the computer's attempt to read a disk in drive A. But there is no disk in drive A, remember? You were supposed to remove any disk in this drive. So you hear a lot of pathetic gronking and grakking until the computer gives up, and goes hunting on your hard disk instead. This is weird and noisy, but normal.

DOS is stored on your hard disk. Your computer needs DOS to run. So what happens if something goes wrong with your hard disk—something minor that could be fixed pretty easily? Your computer accesses drive A first so that, if your hard disk won't respond, you can put a DOS disk in drive A and get your system going. From there, you can find out whether there's something seriously wrong with your hard disk or just a minor glitch.

"I HATE THIS!"

"It says, Non-system disk or disk error!"

Congratulations. Despite my having harped on this repeatedly, you left a disk in drive A, didn't you? Remove the disk, and restart your system by pressing the Reset button. (If your computer doesn't have a Reset button, hold down the Ctrl and Alt keys, and then press the Del key.)

Loading DOS

Assuming all has gone well, your computer now finds DOS on your hard disk (which is called *drive C*), and you may see the message `Starting MS-DOS`. This goes pretty smoothly and automatically, but then all hell breaks loose on-screen and dozens of incomprehensible messages flash by. These messages come from the *system configuration files*, things that DOS wizards create to set up your system for the best possible operation. They're pretty techy, and you can ignore them.

BUZZWORDS

LOAD

To take a program from the disk and put it in the computer's memory, where you can work with it.

If you're gonna have a crash, here's where it might just happen. Any errors in these system configuration file things will cause problems, including causing your system to crash. If your computer goes comatose at this point, get your local DOS wizard to come have a look.

Note: A little C> or C:\> on-screen is normal; it doesn't signal that your system is comatose. Instead, it tells you that DOS is ready to do what you want. If you see this, all has gone well.

What Now?

Your system might have been configured by someone else. There are hundreds of ways to configure a system, so I can't tell you exactly what will appear on-screen. I can make a couple guesses. So I'll do that. The two most likely outcomes are that you'll see MS-DOS or Microsoft Windows.

BUZZWORDS

CONFIGURE

To customize a computer system or program so that certain options are in effect. For example, you can configure a computer so that Microsoft Windows starts automatically when you switch on the power.

What might happen after you start the system

▼ Probably, you'll see a tiny C> or C:\> on an otherwise-blank screen. This means your computer has been configured to run DOS. Turn to Chapter 3.

▼ A real possibility: After a lot of thrashing of the disk, you may see a pretty picture showing some house-type windows, lots of color (assuming you have a color monitor, of course), and,

continues

31

What might happen after you start the system, continued

finally, a box called Program Manager. This means your computer has been configured to run Microsoft Windows. Skip the next chapter and delve right into Chapter 4.

▼   Less likely: A program may start. If so, find out how to exit the program and return to DOS. Ask coworkers, call your local DOS guru, or in the extreme, pull out the program's manual.

▼   Even less likely: You might see something called the DOS Shell. If so, press the F3 key (that's one of those funny function keys that runs along the top of the keyboard). This gets you back to DOS; now turn to Chapter 3 to find out how to whip DOS into shape.

▼   You might see a menu, which tells you which key(s) to press to start a program. This is good. You are lucky. Someone has set up the system to make things easy for you. Just press the indicated number or letter to start a program.

Top Ten Least Popular Startup Error Messages

10. Disk destroyed. Destroy another (Y/N)?

9. Qualified user not found. Find qualified user and press any key when ready

8. System tired of reading drive C; drive no longer valid

7. Go ahead. Make my day (Y/N)?

6. Self-destruct sequence initiated. Two minutes to detonation. Counting.

5. Fatal error. Job killed. Authorities notified.

4. Wrong disk error reading drive A. Insert finger in disk drive for punishment.

3. System configuration error. Software boring. Insert Wheel of Fortune software program and press any key when ready.

2. Whole world unfair to computers. System on strike.

1. Hi. This is a computer virus. I've erased all your work. Have fun retyping it. Bye, now!

CHAPTER 3

Read This If You See C:/>, C>, or Some Variation

IN A NUTSHELL

▼ What the DOS prompt is

▼ How to start a program

▼ What to do if the program doesn't start

▼ How to tell what's on a disk

▼ How to exit a program

▼ How to turn off the computer

▼ How to restart your computer

I HATE PCs!

I f you've started your computer and see a C>, C:\>, or some variation on-screen, your computer has been set up to start DOS. DOS is one of the necessary evils of computing. This chapter shows you how to pull off the very basic maneuvers of using DOS and DOS programs. For more on DOS, skip ahead to Chapter 15.

The DOS Prompt, Beloved by Millions. Not!

Chances are, when you turn on your computer, you see this on-screen:

    c:\>

This is the infamous DOS prompt.

HUH?

BUZZWORDS

DOS PROMPT

This C:\> thing is called the *DOS prompt*. It means that DOS is telling you, "We've finished all of our business inside the computer, here. What do you want to do?" To make something happen, you type a few characters and press Enter.

Checklist

▼ Your prompt might say something like Hey, Babe. DOS technoweenies know how to change the prompt to say anything they like. It could even be something silly like, I must obey my master. What is thy bidding?

▼ If you're dying to make DOS prompt you with some goofy message, type **PROMPT**, press the space bar, and then type the message that you want DOS to display. Then press Enter. Your change will

36

only affect the current session—DOS forgets it when you switch off the computer or reboot. That's good, because you'll probably get sick of it pretty fast.

▼ You might see a menu, which tells you which key(s) to press to start a program. This is good. You are lucky. Someone has set up the system to make things easy for you. Just press the indicated number or letter to start a program.

"I HATE THIS!"

My mouse doesn't work!

Your computer system may be equipped with a mouse, a little soap-sized thing that you can move around on the tabletop. Some DOS applications use the mouse, but the DOS prompt doesn't. If you move the mouse while the DOS prompt is visible, nothing good happens. On the plus side, though, nothing bad happens.

Running a Program

(The rocket launch)

You've started your computer, and you see the DOS prompt. So what do you do now? You *run a program*. (Computer people don't agree on what this should be called. You may hear the term *start*, which is simple enough, but you may run into *launch* or even *invoke*. Personally, I like the term launch, because it makes it sound as if you have done something big and exciting like launching a Thor or Atlas missile.)

Here's how to start a program: type the program's name and press Enter. It doesn't matter whether you use uppercase or lowercase letters. For example, to start Lotus 1-2-3, you type **123** and press Enter. (Pressing Enter confirms what you've typed, and sends it to the computer's "brain.") The Enter key is usually the biggest key on the keyboard, so it's hard to miss. It's where the Return key would be on a typewriter.

The following table lists what you type to start some of the most popular programs. You can't start any of these, though, unless they're installed on your computer. Ask the person who set up the system for you whether there are any programs installed, and if so, what you type to start them.

To start:	Type this and press Enter:
dBASE IV	**DBASE**
Harvard Graphics	**HG**
Microsoft Windows	**WIN**
Microsoft Word for DOS	**WORD**
Microsoft Word for Windows	**WINWORD**
ProComm Plus	**PCPLUS**
Q & A	**QA**
Quattro Pro for DOS	**Q**
Quicken	**Q**
WordPerfect for DOS	**WP**
WordStar	**WS**

Checklist

▼ If you start Windows, Windows takes over and DOS makes itself scarce. (It's still there, actually, making things difficult for you at an unseen level.) Turn to the next chapter, which delves into the brave new world of Windows computing.

▼ If your computer doesn't have any application programs yet, see Chapter 18 to learn about installing software (copying programs from the program disks to your hard disk).

▼ What if you make a typing mistake? Before you press Enter, you can correct the mistake by pressing the Backspace key. (Look for the Backspace key above the big Enter key. Sometimes the Backspace key isn't labeled Backspace, but instead has a left arrow on it.) Pressing Backspace rubs out what you've typed—one character at a time—so that you can correct the error by retyping.

Top Ten Reasons for Calling Technical Support Hotline

10. Manual further away than telephone; prefer to let fingers do the walking

9. Manual too hard to read; not interesting like *National Enquirer*

8. Manual buried under three pounds of memos outlining new office efficiencies

7. Unable to start program

6. Unable to exit program

5. Program? What's a program?

continues

I HATE PCs!

Top Ten Reasons for Calling Technical Support Hotline, continued

4. Error beep too loud; audible by coworkers

3. Heard moaning sound from disk drive after installing program

2. Lonely; "just wanted to chat"

1. Apology demanded for insulting error message

I've Got Those Error Message Blues

You typed your program's name or initials and you pressed Enter. And what do you get for following instructions? Something like this:

```
Bad command or file name
```

If you get this message, there are several possible causes. Start with this one: you may have typed the program name or initials wrong. Make sure that you know exactly what to type, and then try again.

If you still get the message, you probably need to switch to the program's directory, as explained in the next section.

You May Need to Change Directories

You may have to activate the program's directory before you can start the program.

BUZZWORDS

DIRECTORY

A *directory* is a section of your disk that has been set aside to store a group of related files, such as the WordPerfect program and your WordPerfect files. Another term for *directory* is *subdirectory*—for now, you can assume that they mean the same thing. (Chapter 14 delves into the subtle and forgettable difference between *directory* and *subdirectory*.)

To activate your program's directory, you need to know its name. Ask the person who set up the computer. If no one's around who can help, you can use the DIR command, as explained in the next section.

After you know the name of the directory, you use the CD command (short for **C**hange **D**irectory) to activate the directory that contains the program you want to start. Suppose that you want to start WordPerfect 5.1, and you learn that this program is in the WP51 directory. Here's what you type:

    CD \WP51

Then press Enter. Note a couple of things here. First, there's a space between the CD part and the \WP51 part. You don't have to type the space. Second, that funny mark is a backslash. Don't leave it out. It tells DOS, "The letters that follow are a directory name."

Your computer may have been set up so that the DOS prompt shows the name of the directory that's currently active. If so, the prompt now looks like this:

    C:\WP51>

But if no one has set up your system to do this, it might just look like this:

    C>

41

You are in the WP51 directory no matter what the prompt says—provided that you typed the directory name correctly. And you should be able to start your program now.

Checklist

▼ If you see the message `Invalid directory`, make sure that you've typed the directory name correctly, and try again. Don't leave out the backslash!

▼ If your prompt doesn't show the name of the current directory, get your local DOS guru to modify it so that it does.

TIP

If you have to change directories before you can start your program, get your local DOS guru to modify your system. The modification's pretty simple. It involves adding something called a PATH command to one of those files DOS consults when you start your system, and it will only take one or two minutes to do. Don't try to do it yourself, though, unless you really want to spend the next 48 hours wading through DOS manuals.

The DIR Command

("What's on this disk?")

When you don't know the name of a program or a directory and can't find out easily any other way, use the DIR command. DIR is one of the DOS commands that you'll use frequently. It lists for you the files and directories that are in the current directory.

BUZZWORDS

FILE

A collection of related stuff stored on disk, such as a program like WordPerfect or Chapter 12 of your latest novel. Every file has its own, unique name, which must conform to DOS's strict regulations about length (8 characters maximum) and which characters you can include. Chapter 14 covers the fascinating topic of files.

To see what's on a disk, type **DIR** and press Enter. You'll see something like this on-screen:

```
Volume in drive C is HOT_STUFF
Volume Serial Number is 0D57-15
Directory of C:\

COMMAND     COM      4785     11-11-91      5:00a
CONFIG      SYS      1536     07-04-92      5:36p
MOUSE       SYS     30733     03-10-92     11:36a
AUTOEXEC    BAT      1876     05-09-92      8:31p
WP51                <DIR>     05-09-92      8:37p
LOTUS               <DIR>     07-30-92     12:19p
```

Don't worry about most of the stuff you're seeing here. You can learn more about it later, if you want. For now, just notice that this command lists the names of the files and directories that are found in the currently active directory. You can tell that something in the list is a directory because <DIR> appears after the name. This listing shows two directories: WP51 and LOTUS.

When you first turn on the computer, the root directory is usually the current directory.

BUZZWORDS

ROOT DIRECTORY

The top-level directory on a disk. Think of the root directory as if it were a country that contains lots of states (other directories).

TIP

If you want to see a list of subdirectories only, type **DIR *.** (an asterisk followed by a period) and press Enter.

Suppose that you're trying to hunt down a program's name or initials so that you can start it. You know that the program is stored in the \123 directory. So you switch to this directory by typing **CD \123** and pressing Enter. \123 is now the current directory.

Now type **DIR *.EXE** and press Enter. (That's DIR, followed by a space, an asterisk, a period, and EXE. Don't put a space in the *.EXE part.) Most program files have the extension or last name EXE. (More on file names and their parts in Chapter 14.)

You see the program files stored in the \123 directory. You'll probably see several programs, and one of them will probably be the one you're after. To start the program, type the part of the name that comes before the period—like the 123 in 123.EXE—and then press Enter.

Making a Graceful Exit

Let's assume all has gone well and that you've started your program successfully. (Granted, this might be a pretty big assumption.) The question now arises: how to get out?

CAUTION

Don't quit a program by just switching off the computer, tempting though it may be. It's much better to exit the program and return to the DOS prompt. There's less risk of losing your work or screwing things up.

It would be nice if all programs gave you the same way to exit. Naturally, they don't. This was decided at a conference titled "Let's Make Things as Difficult as Possible for Our Users," held in the dawning years of the computer industry.

To exit, try one of the following:

▼ If the program has a bar across the top of the screen with names of menus like File and Edit, you can probably exit by holding down the Alt key (one of those funny extra keys on the keyboard) and pressing F. This command opens the File menu. Tap the down-arrow key until you highlight the command that gets you out of the program—Exit, Quit, Die, and so on. If you don't see such a bar, press F10 and see whether one appears.

▼ In Lotus 1-2-3, press the slash key (/) and then tap the right-arrow key until you move the highlight to the command called Quit. Then press Enter, followed by Y for Yes.

▼ To quit Quattro Pro, hold down the Ctrl key and press X.

▼ To quit Q & A, press X at the main menu to choose X - Exit.

▼ Some programs give you a list of keys you can press to do various things. Usually, this list is at the bottom of the screen. In one program, the list says `F3=Quit`. If you press F3, you exit the program.

CHAPTER 3

▼ If the program is WordPerfect, press F7. You are asked whether you want to save the document. Press N if you don't or Y if you do. Then press Y when asked whether you're really serious about leaving the program. No other program uses this key to exit, though, which is one of WordPerfect's most beloved little peculiarities.

Turning Off Your Computer

Now that you've exited your program gracefully and returned to the DOS prompt, you may want to turn off your computer. To turn off your computer, remove any floppy disks you may have inserted, and then flip off the power strip, if you have one. If you don't, flip off the power switches for the computer, monitor, and printer.

CAUTION

It's OK to leave a frequently used computer on all the time, but turn off the monitor. If you leave the monitor on, you'll get burn-through—a permanent image left on-screen by whatever is left on-screen for a prolonged period (such as the DOS prompt). You might have noticed burn-through on automatic teller machines where the Welcome screen seems to appear as a ghost image on-screen no matter what screen you are viewing.

Another way to avoid burn-through is to use a screen-saver program, discussed in Chapter 8. These programs blank the screen after a set period—say, 10 or 15 minutes—in which you haven't typed anything or moved the mouse.

Restarting the Computer

You may want to restart your computer—to take it back to that magic moment when its memory is cleared and DOS is loaded for a new, fresh computing session. You can do so without switching the power off and on, which decreases your computer's life span. Hold down the Ctrl and Alt keys and press Del. Alternatively, press your computer's Reset button—if your computer has one. (If it does, you'll find it on the computer's front panel.)

When should you restart your system? These are some of the pertinent times:

▼ When a software installation program instructs you to do so. Installation programs change your computer's setup, and the new setup won't take place until you restart.

▼ If your system *crashes*, *hangs*, or *freezes* (something has gone haywire so that the computer no longer responds to your keyboard input). Be sure that your computer really *is* frozen. Some operations can take a minute or two to finish, so it appears that your computer is hanging, when really it's just working more slowly than you expected. If any light on the computer is flashing, the computer is still busy. If you hear any computer-related noises, it's probably still working. Go have a cup of cappuccino and come back. If the system's still comatose, restart it.

CAUTION

When you restart your system, you lose any work that you haven't yet saved. Use Ctrl+Alt+Del only as a last-ditch measure, after you've exhausted all other possibilities—including getting your local computer guru to help. And be sure to remove any floppy disks before you restart. (If a disk is left in the drive, you'll probably get an error message when you restart.)

CHAPTER 4

Read This If You See "Program Manager"

IN A NUTSHELL

- ▼ What Windows is and why so many people like it
- ▼ What Program Manager does
- ▼ What a GUI is
- ▼ How to use a mouse
- ▼ How to handle basic Windows maneuvers
- ▼ How to run a Windows application
- ▼ How to switch from one application to another
- ▼ How to exit a Windows application
- ▼ How to quit Microsoft Windows

I HATE PCs!

I f you see a box on-screen labeled Program Manager, your system has been configured to run Microsoft Windows automatically. Unlike those poor, struggling DOS users, you'll be able to choose options by moving the mouse pointer to little pictures on-screen and clicking the mouse button. As you work with your applications, you'll see your document on-screen just as it will appear when printed.

Chapter 16 discusses the ins and outs of managing files with Windows. Here, you learn how to get your program started, switch from your program to other programs, and exit Windows in one piece.

Why Windows?

In case you've spent the last five years in the wilds of the Northwest Territories, here's a tip: Windows is sweeping personal computerdom off its C> prompt. Windows makes PCs easier to use.

Windows improves on DOS. DOS doesn't include any standards for how programs will operate, so people designing the programs are on their own. Someone designing a spreadsheet might decide to make the F1 key the Help key. Someone designing a word processing program might decide to make the F3 key the Help key. The programs don't look alike on-screen (called the *user interface*) and you don't run them the same way. Consequently, every time you learn a new DOS program, you have to learn everything, rather than build on what you learned in another DOS program.

Windows, on the other hand, provides a standard look to all its programs. Once you learn how to use Word for Windows, you will have a strong foundation to build on when you want to learn another Windows program like Quattro Pro for Windows. The basic skills you learn in one program, like how to save a file or adjust the size of an on-screen box

(called a *window*), will work in another program. This makes Windows and Windows applications a lot easier to learn and use than DOS programs. Windows users tend to use more programs, not surprisingly.

▼ To run Windows well, you need at least a 386SX computer or better (386DX or, preferably, a zippy 486). Windows runs on a 286, but without certain snazzy features. It doesn't do anything worth writing home about for an 8088/8086 computer. (For information on what all these awful numbers mean, turn to the next chapter.)

▼ To get the most out of Windows, you need *Windows applications*— programs that are specifically designed to work with Windows.

▼ Windows will run DOS programs. Lots of people use Windows with a combination of new, spiffy Windows applications and old, clunky DOS programs.

▼ Why is it called "Windows"? You'll see when you start it. The screen contains lots of boxes—called *windows*—that you can independently move and size. You can hide them or display them, stack them on top of each other, make some big and some small—whatever you want. You can have lots of windows on-screen at the same time so that you can switch quickly from one type of activity to another. For example, in one window you can schedule a meeting on your daily calendar, and then quickly switch to a calculator in another window so that you can balance your checkbook.

▼ *Windows* with a capital *W* refers to Microsoft Windows, the program. The word *windows*, with a lowercase *w*, refers to the on-screen boxes.

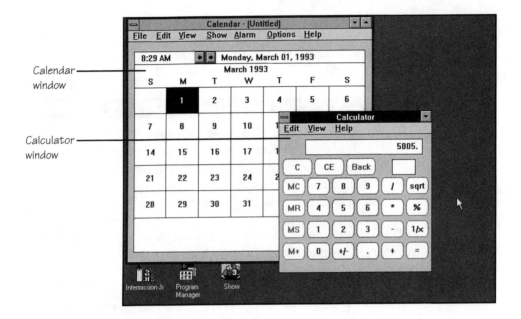

Calendar window

Calculator window

TIP

In the pages to follow, sit down at your computer and try using the mouse. Many of the instructions you'll see, like "move the pointer to the program's icon, and double-click on the left mouse button" take longer to say than to do. You'll learn these procedures quickly.

What's Program Manager? Where's Windows?

When Windows starts, you don't see anything labeled *Windows*, apart from some cool opening graphics. Instead, you see a big window labeled *Program Manager*.

Program Manager starts automatically when Windows starts. Basically, Program Manager is a tool or assistant that you can use to start and organize your Windows applications. Program Manager is like Windows Grand Central Station: it's the starting point for working with Windows, and you come back to it when you want to start other applications or quit Windows.

Program Manager's main function is to help you start an application program. The following shows what you're likely to see when Windows starts (your screen will look different, though, because you have different applications):

The Program
Manager window.

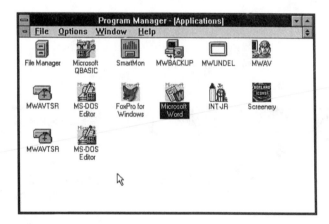

"I HATE THIS!"

I have Windows. Why do I see that ugly DOS prompt?

If you are lucky, Windows starts automatically, and you can avoid that pesky DOS prompt. If you don't see the Program Manager, but are pretty sure you have Windows, you can start Windows yourself. Type the following and press Enter:

WIN

"I HATE THIS!"

Windows should start. If it doesn't, get the help of a computer guru to make sure that indeed you do have Windows and figure out why it won't start. You might also plead with the guru to modify your system so that Windows starts automatically.

What Do You Mean, This is Gooey?

If this is the first time you've seen Program Manager, congratulations! You've had your first encounter with the Brave New World of the graphical user interface.

BUZZWORDS

GRAPHICAL USER INTERFACE (GUI)

This term refers to a way of designing computer programs so that they are easier to use. The program uses on-screen pictures (*icons*) to represent commonly-used computer procedures. Believe it or not, this acronym really is pronounced "gooey."

Checklist

▼ You see windows in a GUI program. (Hey, I bet that's where they got the name for Microsoft Windows!)

▼ Behind the window(s) is the *desktop*. This is the background of the screen, and the windows are positioned on the desktop.

▼ The mouse plays a big role in a GUI program. The easiest way to use Windows is to use the mouse. If you don't have a mouse, or don't like using one, there are keyboard equivalents for most actions. I'll emphasize the mouse techniques here, with an occasional nod to a keyboard substitute that's worth knowing.

▼ GUI programs also make use of pull-down menus. From these menus, you can choose the commands and options available in the program.

▼ This list pretty much sums up the basics of using Windows: working with windows, manipulating a mouse, and using pull-down menus. That's all you really need to know to use Windows. The next sections go into the specifics.

Handy Guide to the Basic Mouse Maneuvers

After you've gotten the hang of the basic mouse maneuvers, you'll feel right at home in Windows. These are the basics:

Name	Maneuver
Point	Move the mouse so that the on-screen pointer moves to something, like an icon. The tip (point) of the mouse pointer needs to be positioned on the item.
Click	Point to something and click the left mouse button. (You will rarely use the right mouse button.)

continues

Name	Maneuver
Double-click	Point to something and press the left mouse button twice in rapid succession.
Drag	Point to something, hold down the left mouse button, and move the mouse. You move (called *dragging*) the item around on the screen. When you've dragged the item to where you want it, release the mouse button.

Windows Calisthenics

(Go for the burn!)

With Program Manager on-screen, you're looking at a certified, bona-fide window (small *w*). The window you see is like all the other windows you'll see in Windows applications. They all have the same parts, so let's take a closer look.

Checklist

▼ To close a window, double-click on the Control menu icon.

▼ To move a window, drag it by the title bar.

▼ The title bar can be used as a clue to which window is active. When the title bar is highlighted (dark), the window is active— that is, the things you do affect this window.

▼ To use a menu, see the next section ("Pull-Down Menu Basics").

▼ To shrink the window to an icon, click on the Minimize button. The icon is placed at the bottom of the screen. To bring the window back to life, double-click on the icon.

▼ To zoom the window to its full size, click on the Maximize button. After zooming the window to full size, you can't resize it. Also, the Maximize window changes, showing arrows pointing both up and down. When you click on the Maximize button in this two-arrow state, Windows restores the window to its previous size.

▼ To resize a window, drag any of its borders.

▼ When there's more stuff in the window than you can see, scroll bars appear. You can scroll in three ways. First, you can click the scroll arrows, which scrolls the window line by line—up, down, left, or right. Second, you can click on either side of the scroll boxes, which scrolls the window about one-third of a windowful per click. Third, you can drag the scroll boxes.

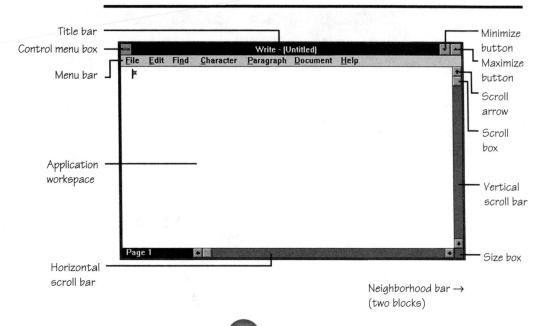

EXPERTS ONLY

Read this if you like to know each and every way to do something

In addition to the quickest method (just described) to work with windows, you also can use the Control menu. Click on the Control menu box to display the Control menu. This menu lets you control the window's size and the location with the keyboard, among other things. Select the command you want.

Pull-Down Menu Basics

Most Windows applications have dozens or even hundreds of command options. To keep the screen uncluttered, they're hidden. To see the commands, you *pull down* a menu (a list of command options) by clicking on the menu.

Pull-down menus contain hidden command options.

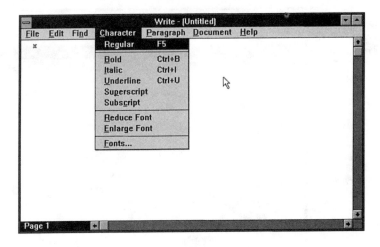

▼ Click the command name again to close the menu.

▼ You can use the keyboard to choose a menu option. Press and hold down the Alt key, and then press the underlined letter in the command name. To close the menu without choosing anything, press Esc. You may have to press Esc more than once.

▼ Some menu options list keyboard shortcuts for command options, like Shift+F5. This means, "Hold down the Shift key and press the F5 key."

▼ Some menu options are followed by three dots, called *ellipses*. These indicate that choosing the option will reveal a *dialog box*. A dialog box is a window that requests even more information from you.

Windows Keyboard Shortcuts

Key or Key Combo	What the Key or Combo Does
Alt or F10	Activates the menu bar
Arrow keys	Moves the highlight to next item
Enter	Chooses whatever's highlighted
Esc	Closes the menu or dialog box without choosing anything
Alt+Tab	Switches applications

continues

Windows Keyboard Shortcuts, continued	
Key or Key Combo	What the Key or Combo Does
Ctrl+Esc	Displays the Task List for task switching
Alt+space bar	Displays the Control menu for the current window
Ctrl+F4	Closes the current window
F1	Gets help
Alt+F4	Quits the current application

"I HATE THIS!"

I punched both keys at once, but it doesn't work!

A lot of beginning users get snarled with keyboard commands like Alt+Esc because they try to pounce on both keys at once. The correct maneuver is a kind of rolling motion, beginning with pressing Alt and, while still holding it down, sweeping up to peck Esc. It's all in the wrist.

And Now Back to Program Manager, Already in Progress

If you look at the bottom part of Program Manager's workspace, you'll probably see several icons. These are *minimized windows*. Try double-clicking on one of them. Lo! A window pops up.

In Program Manager, these windows `are called *program groups*. A program group window contains icons for a bunch of related programs. For example, you probably have an Accessories program group. (Windows created this program group when you or someone else installed the program.)

TIP

If a program group window is hiding a minimized icon, preventing you from opening it, you have two options. First, you can minimize the big, bloated window that's preventing you from seeing what's under it. That will teach it! Second, you can open any program group window by choosing its name from the Window menu.

Tile and Cascade

(These are not detergents)

When you get a lot of windows on-screen, it's hard to see the ones underneath. For this reason, Windows provides a couple of features called *tiling* and *cascading*.

To try tiling and cascading, open lots of program group windows by clicking on all the minimized icons at the bottom of the Program Group workspace. Move open windows up and out of the way, if necessary, so that you can click even more icons. (To move a window, drag the title bar.)

Now click on the Window menu name, and from the pull-down menu, click on Cascade. (As a shortcut to this rather lengthy procedure, just press Shift+F5.) As you can see, the windows are nicely "cascaded" so you can see each window's title bar.

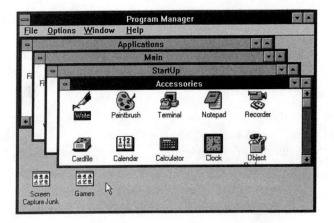

Cascaded windows.

Now choose the Tile option from the Window menu, or press Shift+F4. Now you get little bitty windows, all jammed together, side by side. But at least you can see each one clearly.

Launching Programs

(5, 4, 3, 2, 1, liftoff!)

In Windows, you don't just start an application. That wouldn't be dramatic enough. You *launch* it. Or *run* it. Or *invoke* it. (The terms all mean the same thing.) You can launch Windows applications, naturally. But you can also launch DOS applications. When a DOS application starts, it takes over the screen, and from then on, you'd never know you were working with Windows—until you quit the DOS application, and Program Manager pops back on-screen.

To run an application, you need to display the program group window that contains the icon of the application. For example, Write, a mini-word processing program, is in the Accessories program group.

Try displaying the Accessories program group window now. (If you can't see it, minimize other groups or choose Accessories from the Window menu.)

To run an application, just double-click on the program icon, and your application is off and running. Try launching Write.

Checklist

▼ When your application is on-screen, a whole new set of capabilities becomes available. If you start Ami Pro for Windows or Word for Windows, for example, you can write, edit, format, and print your work. If you start Quattro Pro for Windows, you can work with numbers and produce handsomely printed reports. These and other software options are covered in Chapter 17.

▼ Even if this is the first time you've laid eyes on your application, you see the familiar window features that you've already learned, such as the pull-down menus, the scroll bars, and more. That's why people like Windows so much—you already know a little bit about how to use this program!

"I HATE THIS!"

My application isn't in any of these darned group windows!

Some applications don't show up in program group windows, for reasons we won't go into here (tempting though it is). You can use Windows to create new application icons, which solves this difficulty, but the procedure is more advanced than this

"I HATE THIS!"

book covers. (See the companion volume, *I Hate Windows*, so you can develop a full, rich hatred for Windows as well as PCs.) In the meantime, you can launch any application on your disk (including DOS applications) by using File Manager. For the specifics, flip to Chapter 16.

Switching Back to Program Manager

What happens to Program Manager when you start an application? It's still there. You can switch back to Program Manager without losing your work in the application that's running.

To switch back to Program Manager, click on the Control menu box to display the Control menu, and then choose the Switch To option. Or press Ctrl+Esc. You then see the Task List dialog box. To switch back to Program Manager, just double-click on Program Manager in the task list.

Now Program Manager pops up over the application you're running. (If the Program Manager window isn't maximized, you can probably see parts of your application in the background.) To switch back to your application, use the Control menu again and choose Switch To, but this time double-click on the application's name in the Task List.

TIP

There are lots of cool shortcuts for switching windows. Try pressing Alt+Tab (hold down the Alt key and press Tab). Keep holding down the Alt key; each time you press Tab, you see a box giving the name of one of the active applications. To choose one, just let go of the Alt key.

TIP

Another technique: minimize the application so that you can see the application underneath it. You can activate this application just by clicking anywhere within the window. The fastest technique of all: If you see part of the other application's window jutting out, click on that part to activate the application.

Why Would You Even Want to Do This Switching Stuff?

Imagine that you've just started Write to type a letter, and then you go back to Program Manager and launch Cardfile, where you keep your name and address files. You can work with one application, and then work with the other, just by switching between them. Pretty cool.

Checklist

▼ One of the nicest things about running two or more applications at once is that you can easily copy or move text or graphics from one application to another.

▼ Another nice thing about running two or more applications at once is that you can start a time-consuming operation, like printing a lengthy document, and then switch to another application and continue working. The printing keeps going while you do other work.

continues

▼ Task switching works with DOS programs, too. If you have a DOS program running, you can press Alt+Tab at any time to get back to Program Manager. (The DOS program is still there, in the background.) You can switch back to it by pressing Alt+Tab again or by choosing the DOS program's name from the Task List.

Exiting a Windows Application

(Get me outta here!)

Now that you've gotten into Windows and explored a bit, learn how to quit a Windows application gracefully. You can do so lots of different ways, but the fastest method is to double-click on the Control menu box for the program window.

"I HATE THIS!"

It's asking me whether I want to save changes!

If you do any "experimental" typing in an application, you see an alert box. This box warns you that your work will be lost unless you save a copy of it to a disk. To do so, click on Yes, and type a file name (the file name can be up to 8 letters and numbers). Then click on the big Save button or press Enter. To abandon your work (let it disappear into the computer equivalent of the Long Dark Night), just click on the No button. To give up the whole thing and go back to your application, click on Cancel.

EXPERTS ONLY

For those gotta-know-it-all type people

You also can exit by clicking on File and then clicking on the Exit option. Or you can press and hold down the Alt key, and then type **FX**. Or press Alt+F4. You can really go nuts trying to remember all these options.

"I HATE THIS!"

I'm stuck!

In Windows, it's easy to get stuck and to think a program has crashed when it really hasn't. A common cause: you accidentally pressed Alt or F10, which activates the menu bar. The program hasn't crashed; it's just waiting for you to select a menu name. To return to your document, press Esc.

Quitting Microsoft Windows

Even if your system starts Windows automatically, you should still exit Windows and return to that DOS prompt before switching off your computer. Why? This is the only way of saving the various working choices you've made since you've been using Windows, such as window size and location. It's a pain, but you really should do it every time you want to quit working—don't just switch off your computer with poor, helpless Windows left on-screen.

To quit Windows, exit all your applications, as described in the previous section. Now click on File, and then click on the Exit Windows command. You also can hold down the Alt key and press F4. You see an alert box informing you that you're about to exit Windows. Click on the OK button, or just press Enter. You see the DOS prompt. *Now* it's safe to shut off your system.

I HATE PCs!

Top Ten Pet Peeves of Computer Mice (If They Could Talk)

10. Choked by own cord

9. Dragged through spilled Pepsi

8. Ridicule over your name. Mouse? Ha. Ha. Ha.

7. When you're left hanging off the desk by your tail

6. Filthy cat hair always gets caught in your mechanism

5. Keyboard feels that it can bully you because of your size

4. Underbelly burn from toddler rubbing you back and forth at break-neck speed over the mouse pad

3. Cup of hot coffee teetering precariously close to you

2. Owner doesn't wash his hands first. Lord knows where they've been.

1. Used as makeshift football for impromptu family scrimmage

PART II

Hardware

Includes:

CHAPTER 5

The System Unit
(Opening Pandora's Box)

IN A NUTSHELL

▼ Brief, relatively painless introduction to the parts of a computer system

▼ What's in the system unit

▼ Explanation of all that 80286, 80386, 80486 chatter

▼ Why faster isn't necessarily better

▼ Why it's great to have a big hard disk

▼ What ports are and how to tell which is which

Hardware is the physical part of the computer: all the drives, screens, boxes, chips, and wires. If it hurts when you drop it on yourself, it's hardware. If you drop it and it doesn't hurt, it could be software. Or maybe you just imagined the whole thing.

The other part of the computer is *software*, which really just means *programs*. Different programs are designed for different tasks. There are programs for serious tasks, like balancing your checkbook or calculating a mortgage. And, yes, there are programs for even more serious tasks, like writing a will. And, as you might have surmised, there are programs for Still More Serious tasks, such as defending Earth from alien invaders, or helping the King on his latest Quest (highly recommended).

But our concern here is with hardware—the vexing and troublesome stuff which, when working right, makes all these wonders possible. You take a closer look at programs in Part III of this book.

This isn't the only chapter in the book that discusses hardware. All the chapters in Part II deal with hardware, one way or another. This chapter delves into the *system unit*, the computer's main box, letting all kinds of technical verbiage spew forth. Fortunately, you need to understand only a few basic terms and concepts to understand whether a given PC is a hopped-up screamer or a deadbeat slowpoke. The rest, thank heavens, you can forget.

The Parts of a Typical System

You can divide a typical IBM or IBM-compatible computer system into two parts: the ones you can see and the ones you can't.

The system's capabilities, wouldn't you know it, are determined largely by the stuff you can't see. It's sort of like the fine print in that "Spend Four Days and Three Nights in Cancun for $19.95" brochure.

The Parts of the System You Can See

Name	Description
System Unit	A big box with one or more slots in the front and lots of plugs in the back. The front panel probably has a Reset button, some lights, and a key, which you can lose so that you won't be able to start your computer. Also called, erroneously but pretty often, the CPU.
Ports	Plugs on the back that you use to connect computer accessories like monitors and printers.
Floppy Disk Drive	One or two slots in the system unit. You insert disks into these slots. Chapter 7 discusses disk drives.
Monitor	The television-type thing. If you're interested in learning about monitors, turn to Chapter 8, which discusses nothing but.
Printer	Box that looks like a copier or a typewriter without a keyboard. Chapter 10 covers the humorous task of getting your printer to actually print something.
Keyboard	Keyboard. This is elaborated on in Chapter 9.

continues

Name	Description
Cord	Cords (lots).
Aspirin	For minor crashes, accidental erasures, stress caused by insulting error messages.

The Parts of the System You Can't See

Name	Description
Power Supply	Converts electrical current into a form the computer can use. The power supply is tucked away inside the system unit. A power supply should have enough muscle to handle your system—a 200 watt power supply is generally considered about right. Really loaded systems might require a 250 watt power supply. The power supply includes a fan, which might be really noisy and irritating.
Motherboard	The mother of all circuit boards inside your computer; contains microprocessor and memory (RAM). Again, this is inside the system unit.
Microprocessor	A tiny, complex plug-in module that contains the computer's processing circuitry. Also called *CPU*, short for *central processing unit*. The "brain" of the computer. Stored inside the system unit.

Name	Description
Memory (RAM)	The place where your programs and data are kept while the microprocessor is working on them. RAM can only be used when the computer is on, which is why the hard disk is necessary. (Flip to Chapter 6 for more information on RAM.) At the beginning of a work session, you *load* programs into memory (that's what happens when you start them).
ROM	This stands for *read-only memory*. In brief, it's a little computer chip that stores very simple programs that help the computer get going. This includes the computer's *BIOS* program (basic input-output system). BIOS comes into play when you turn on your system, as you learn in Chapter 2.
Hard Disk	A disk that stores DOS, your programs, and your data when you're not using them or when the computer is off. The hard disk is stored inside the system unit and can hold lots and lots of data. Hard disks are briefly discussed in this chapter, but see Chapter 7 for the lowdown.
Expansion Boards	Plug-in circuit boards (also called *adapters*) that add capabilities such as sound to your computer system. There are probably several of these already installed to handle stuff like your monitor.

continues

Name	Description
Expansion Slots	Receptacles for the expansion boards. Chances are that you have several empty slots inside your computer's case. Sticking stuff into these slots is pretty tricky; leave this job for a pro.
Drive Bays	Openings that a technician can use to install additional disk drives or tape backup units. Chances are that your computer has one or more drive bays. Your floppy disk drive and hard disk are taking up two of them.
Bus	The wiring grid to which the computer's internal components are attached. The faster the bus, the faster the computer.

"I HATE THIS!"

I have to learn all this stuff?

No, thank goodness. What determines your system's capabilities are the following: the microprocessor and its *clock speed*, the capacity of its hard disk, and the amount of memory that's installed. The first two of these three momentous topics receive attention in the following sections; memory gets its own, fat chapter. After discussing the microprocessor and hard disk capacity, the rest of the chapter deals with stuff you can skip if you like.

CAUTION

Don't block the fan! If you stack stuff up against the back of your computer so that it can't breathe, you raise the possibility that the fan won't operate efficiently enough to cool critical components. This can lead to computer failures and some very expensive repairs.

A Quick Guide to All That "80286, 80386, 80486" Chatter

You've probably seen that cool Intel ad on TV where the camera is like a tiny spaceship, going in through the disk drive door and zooming around until it finds, first, the motherboard, and then—Lo!—the microprocessor. The ad is correct in placing so much emphasis on the microprocessor. The microprocessor is the one component that, more than any other, determines your computer's capabilities, such as how fast it can work and what kind of software it can run.

One of the most confusing things about PCs for beginners is that there are so many different microprocessor model numbers. Intel gives each microprocessor a distinctive model number, the way Boeing numbers its airplanes. As time goes on, Intel Corporation, which makes the microprocessors used in IBM and IBM-compatible computers, keeps making improvements. Basically, the larger the number, the greater the capabilities—an 80486 is better than an 80386.

I HATE PCs!

EXPERTS ONLY

"And how do you pronounce that, Sir?"

"Eight-oh-three-eight-six" is hard to say, so people just say "three-eighty-six" or "four-eighty-six." The cool way to write this is '386 or '486. Nobody talks about 8088s or 8086s, though, out of respect for the dead. Incidentally, it is considered an extreme social faux pas to enter a computer store and loudly announce, "Please show me an eighty-thousand-three-hundred-eighty-six, if you don't mind."

Here's a quick guide to the microprocessors that drive the machines you're likely to encounter. You'll notice that these microprocessors are evaluated in terms of how well they run Microsoft Windows, which is discussed in Chapters 4 and 16.

TIP

Windows (and Windows programs) are clearly the wave of the future, but millions of people are content to run DOS and DOS programs. For these people, these old, obsolete microprocessors are just fine, thank you.

Model Number	Nickname	Snap Assessment
8088	XT or Turbo XT	The original (circa 1981) microprocessor of the IBM PC. Still serviceable, but very slow by today's standards. Won't run Microsoft Windows programs.

Model Number	Nickname	Snap Assessment
8086	XT or Turbo XT	A slightly faster version of the 8088, but still woefully clunky by today's standards. Won't run Windows programs. A more recent low-power version called the 80C86 is found in some cheap notebook or palmtop computers. (Flip to Chapter 13 for more information about portable computers.)
80286	286 or AT	Introduced in 1984 with a computer called the IBM AT (Advanced Technology), this microprocessor runs faster and can use more memory than its predecessors. However, it has technical limitations that prevent it from taking full advantage of Microsoft Windows and Windows programs.

continues

Model Number	Nickname	Snap Assessment
80386DX	386DX	A technical knockout, this speedy, capable microprocessor is ideal for using Microsoft Windows and Windows programs.
80386SX	386SX	A junior version of the 386DX; sacrifices some speed so that it can use cheaper (but slower) components, such as disk drives. Runs Windows a bit sluggishly. Today this is considered the entry-level microprocessor.
80486DX	486DX	The top-of-the-line microprocessor *right now* (technology grows at lightning speed, so this information could be outdated tomorrow). An awesome microprocessor that shows what Microsoft Corporation has in mind for Windows. Sometimes this processor is numbered i486 (the *i* standing for Intel).

I HATE PCs!

Model Number	Nickname	Snap Assessment
80486DX2	486DX2	A version of the 486DX that runs twice as fast as the rest of the computer.
80486SX	486SX	A junior version of the 486DX, but almost as fast—except in the case of heavy-duty number crunching.
Pentium	586	Intel's newest and snazziest chip. Why did they call it *Pentium*? It's a long story, and even more boring than most of the stuff in this list, so I think I'll just skip it.

BUZZWORDS

MATH COPROCESSOR

An additional circuit that helps the computer work with numbers more quickly. If you plan to do a lot of number crunching, you might want to add a math coprocessor to your system. This can be done when you order your computer, or later. 486DX systems have a built-in math coprocessor.

Timing Clock Speed

(On your mark, get set, go)

"My 386 is running at 33 megahertz," your colleague says, proudly. But you're not sure whether this assertion is good or bad. Well, rest assured; your colleague probably doesn't either. The speed at which a microprocessor runs, called *clock speed* and measured in megahertz (MHz), is one of the most misunderstood measurements of a computer's capabilities.

BUZZWORDS

MEGAHERTZ

The term *megahertz* (MHz) refers to "one million cycles per second," which seems like a lot, but computers have a lot of data to crunch. The faster, the better.

Why is clock speed misunderstood? Because these speeds aren't easily compared from one microprocessor to another. Here's why: A great, big power backhoe shoveling 20 shovel loads in 10 minutes will shovel a lot more dirt than a teeny hand shovel, even if the poor shoveler can shovel 200 shovel loads a minute. Likewise, a 486 running at 20 megahertz is faster than a 386 running at 33 megahertz. But most people do not know that. Most people do not *care*.

Clock speeds aren't a reliable guide to system performance when you are comparing two different microprocessors. But when you're comparing two systems that use the same microprocessor, they are.

I HATE PCs!

Here's a quick, no-details bluffer's guide to clock speeds:

Speed	Snap Assessment
4.77 MHz	Like walking through sand
8 MHz	Cold molasses
12 MHz	Lukewarm molasses
16 MHz	Barely tolerable
20 MHz	Not bad
25 MHz	Better; there's a genuine zip to it
33 MHz	Very satisfyingly zippy
50 MHz	A screamer; wish mine did 50
60 MHz	A rocket; awesome

Checklist

▼ If you're planning to run DOS and only DOS programs, you don't need as much speed. 16 MHz might be plenty in a 386DX.

▼ If you think you might run Microsoft Windows, you need all the speed you can get.

EXPERTS ONLY

Detailed technical babble
about busses that you'd be wise to skip

Another thing that affects a computer's speed is its *bus*, the network of wires that connects all those plug-in expansion boards. Most clones use what's called the *Industry Standard Architecture* (ISA) bus, which is OK for most purposes. You need something better than ISA only if you're using Windows and doing a lot of work with graphics (photographs, movies, architectural design, and the like).

You have three choices beyond ISA:

▼ Extended Industry Standard Architecture (EISA) bus (found in some clones)

▼ BM's PS/2 computers with the Micro Channel Architecture (MCA) bus

▼ The latest in bus technologies, the *local bus*, which sounds like the municipal transit route that runs from the K-Mart to the state hospital. But it's the tippity-tops in processing speed.

Isn't this boring? Most users will be quite happy with the ISA bus that comes in your average clone.

Hard Disk

(There's no such thing as enough hard disk space)

The last hidden system unit thing that determines your system's capabilities is the capacity of your hard disk drive.

What's a disk drive? A *disk drive* is like a cassette recorder that uses round cassettes (*disks*). Only rather than play and record music, the drive *reads* (puts information into the memory) and *writes* (stores information back on the disk).

In floppy disk drives—the ones you see slots for on the outside of the system unit—you can insert floppy disks into the drive. Without a disk in the drive, the drive is useless—just like you can't play music from a cassette player without inserting a cassette.

In a hard drive, though, the disk is built in. That's why the whole thingamajig is located inside the system unit—there's no need to get your hot little hands on it. Hard disks have lots more storage space, and they operate much faster than floppy drives.

Most computers have two disk drives: one hard and one floppy. Some have three drives: one hard and two floppy. A few computers even have two or more hard drives or three or more floppy disk drives.

In general, the more capacity your hard disk has, the happier you'll be with your PC. You use your hard disk to store all the application programs, as well as the work that you do with your computer. The more space you have, the less chance you'll run out. (Running out of space is a real pain.) When you run out of space, you have to move some programs or data files off the disk, which means they aren't so readily accessible when you want to use them.

The details of measuring hard disk capacity are discussed in Chapter 7, but a few notes here are warranted. I have, after all, raised the subject. A few years ago, it was considered a very big deal to have a 40 megabyte (MB) hard disk. (The term *megabyte* refers to roughly one million characters of storage capacity, so a 40MB drive can store roughly 40 million characters. A *character*, by the way, is a letter or number.) But nowadays many people feel that 120MB is the practical minimum, especially if you're running Windows. Windows programs really hog the disk space— oink, oink.

▼ With a floppy disk drive, you have the drive and the disk that you insert into the drive. With a hard disk drive, the disk and the drive are locked into a sealed unit. That's why you might hear the terms *hard disk*, *hard drive*, and *hard disk drive*. These terms all mean the same thing. Some people just give up and call their hard disks Eduardo or Penelope ("Penny").

▼ If you're using a 386 or 486, your system probably has a hard disk with an *IDE* interface. The IDE interface is the standard way of connecting the hard disk to the computer in most of today's clones. Some drives have somewhat faster interfaces that use different methods of linking the drive to the computer, but we're well into the category of forgettable stuff here.

EXPERTS ONLY

Technical minutia about access speed that only a toolie could love

Hard disks vary in speed, too. The faster the disk, the faster things go on-screen. The most widely-quoted measurement of hard disk speed is *access speed*, the time it takes the disk drive mechanism to find data and start feeding it back to the computer. Real slow drives are rated in the 50 to 60 micro-seconds (millionths of a second, abbreviated ms) range; very fast drives are rated in the 9 to 17ms range.

Ports o' Call

A *port* is a plug, on the back of your computer's case, through which you can connect the computer to accessory devices, such as printers. (There are more electronics inside, though, that are linked to these plugs and

handle the linkage to the computer.) There are two types of ports: serial and parallel. You don't have to worry about these things, unless you're unfortunate enough to have to hook up something like a printer.

"I HATE THIS!"

We wouldn't want things to be too simple, would we?

If you look at the back of your computer, you see that the ports aren't labeled. Isn't that nice? This makes it impossible to tell which is which without getting some help. As you see in this section, you can tell the difference yourself if you're willing to inquire into the sensitive subject of whether the plug is *male* (has pins sticking out) or *female* (has holes for male cables).

Checklist

▼ The parallel port is designed for printers. It has 25 holes ready for the male end of the printer cable.

▼ You can use a serial port for printers, modems, scanners, and neat stuff like that. The serial port plug has either 25 or 9 male pins, all ready for a female cable.

▼ The monitor cable goes to a plug that looks deceptively like a 9-pin serial port, except that the plug has 9 female holes for a 9-pin male cable.

▼ Your mouse might be plugged into a 9-pin serial port, or into a special, round plug with 9 pins.

▼ Your keyboard is plugged into a round port with 5 pins.

▼ That pink lump on the back is actually a piece of bubble gum that somebody stuck there when the boss walked in suddenly.

CHAPTER 5

Top Ten Things Overheard in a Hardware Design Lab

10. "Cool! They'll *never* figure this out!"

9. "So what if it takes up the whole desk? They're gonna do all their work with the computer now, anyway."

8. "The heck with that last test. *Seinfeld* is starting."

7. "I keep forgetting—is the female connector the one with the holes or the one with the pins?"

6. "The money we save on all that radiation reduction stuff can go into marketing, you know."

5. "Why don't we put the power switch *under* the case? That way, there's no chance they could shut off the power by accident."

4. "Is it *still* crashing? Well, fudge the report. I'm sick of fooling with it."

3. "Oh, *that* specification? We just made it up."

2. "Hey, look what happens when I pour my Coke into this power supply."

1. "Sorry, we can't finish this job until you buy us the *really* big Erector set."

CHAPTER 6

More Than You Ever Wanted to Know about Memory (RAM)

IN A NUTSHELL

- ▼ Why you need memory at all
- ▼ How memory is measured
- ▼ How much memory you need
- ▼ Why there are different types of memory
- ▼ How to determine how much memory you have
- ▼ How to add more memory
- ▼ How to configure memory

Suppose that you're going to cook up something delicious. From your pantry, cabinets, and cupboards, you assemble the stuff you need, and place it on the countertop. There, it's accessible as you work. (It would take a lot longer if you had to retrieve each item when needed from the pantry, wouldn't it?)

You can think of memory as the countertop. Memory is where you put stuff that you're working with. And you can think of your hard disk as the cabinet storage space, where you store what you aren't using now but may need later. There's a lot more hard disk space than memory, just as there's a lot more cabinet space than countertop space.

TIP

Be sure to remember the distinction between memory (RAM) and disk space. A shortage in one doesn't necessarily mean there's a shortage in the other! "Oh, Dad, I was trying to run Word, and it said there wasn't enough memory. So I deleted a whole bunch of your files from the disk." If DOS says there isn't enough memory to run a program, you need more memory, not more disk space.

What's the Purpose of Memory, Anyway?

Memory is a lot faster than your hard disk. When your computer is working with your programs and data, speed is the keynote. That's why your computer puts your programs and data in memory while you're working with them.

▼ Technoid types like myself like to call memory *RAM*. You hear this term a lot—as in "How much RAM do *you* have?" (RAM, incidentally, stands for *random-access memory*.) RAM and *memory* are synonymous. Other terms for memory are *primary memory* and *internal memory*. They all mean the same thing.

▼ When you start a computer session, you start a program, such as WordPerfect. DOS transfers a copy of the program from your hard disk to RAM. This is called *loading*. Then you start working on something—or retrieve a file from the hard disk. This work goes into RAM, too. Your program and data are both in RAM, together. They get to know each other very well while they're crammed in there.

▼ RAM has one very, very unfortunate drawback: it's *volatile*. No, this doesn't mean that it has a short-fuse personality. It means something far worse, actually. It means that you lose all your data if there's a sudden power loss. RAM needs power to maintain the data stored in it.

▼ Because RAM is volatile, you need to *save your work to disk*, as computer people put it. Disks don't need power to keep the data— after you save (that is, transfer your work from RAM to your disk), you can turn off your computer without wiping out your work.

▼ Do you have enough counter space in your kitchen? Probably not. There's *never* enough counter space. RAM is the same way. There's no such thing as enough memory. That's particularly true if you're running Windows.

I HATE PCs!

CHAPTER 6

EXPERTS ONLY

Read this only if you demand to know what "random access" means

Why do they call it *random access?* It has nothing to do with "random." Here's what this distinction is really all about. A cassette tape has *sequential access*—you have to wind through all the songs, in a sequence, before you get to hear Johnny Mathis sing, "Misty." A CD player, in contrast, has *random access*—you just punch the number of the song you want, and the device goes right to it, with no further ado. In a random-access device, you can directly access what you want, without going through a sequence of stuff. That's why it's a lot faster.

The Art and Lore of Measuring Memory

Memory is measured the same way as hard disk space. In fact, one of the most basic mistakes a beginner (and even a not-so-beginner) makes is to confuse memory and hard disk space. Remember that hard disk space is permanent storage (like cabinet space), and there's a lot of that. Memory is not permanent; it keeps stuff you are working on (think of counter space). There's less space in memory.

Term and Abbreviation	Approximately	Exactly
Byte	One character	8 bits
Kilobyte (K or KB)	One thousand characters	1,024 bytes

Term and Abbreviation	Approximately	Exactly
Megabyte (M or MB)	One million characters	1,048,576 bytes
Gigabyte (G or GB)	One billion characters	1,073,741,824 bytes

Why the difference between "approximately" and "exactly"? Computers are like Noah—they count everything in twos. That's where you get the "exactly" figure. We humans count things in tens—which is just fine, thank you. That's the "approximately" figure, which is close enough.

Checklist

▼ Memory is one of those hidden things inside the system unit, discussed in Chapter 5. The existing memory is found in the form of *memory chips*, little things that resemble black bugs and that are installed on the motherboard.

▼ The amount of memory you have depends on the number of memory chips installed in your computer.

▼ There is probably room on your motherboard for adding more memory. Most computers come with just enough memory to seem competitive. The inside of the computer case probably contains empty places where you can add more memory chips. Computers do limit the amount of memory that you can add; this limit depends on your computer model.

▼ Why should you care about measuring memory? Some programs require more memory than others. Do you have enough? This is the burning question that motivates computer users to learn the art and lore of memory management.

CHAPTER 6

How Much Memory Do You Need?

This one's pretty easy: you need enough to run your programs.

Most DOS programs require 640K, and you should have at least this amount. If you don't have 640K, upgrade your system to that level.

Windows programs, though, require *humongous* amounts of memory—at least 2MB, but 4MB is necessary to run some memory-hungry Windows programs. If you're planning to run Windows, my advice is to upgrade your system, if necessary, with at least 4MB of RAM—8MB, if your budget and your motherboard allow.

A program's memory requirements are usually listed right on the program box. Look for an area called "System Requirements." PC Tools Version 7.1, for example, requires 640K of RAM. To run PC Tools, you need at least 640K of RAM.

Why So Many Kinds of Memory?

Ideally, a computer would have just three kinds of memory: the amount of memory you have, the amount your programs need, and the additional amount you have to add to run your programs. Unfortunately, DOS computers have several different kinds of memory, called horrible things like *conventional memory*, *upper memory*, *high memory*, *extended memory*, *loss of memory*, and more. The two most important terms to understand are *conventional memory* and *extended memory*. You need to understand these terms if you want or need to upgrade your memory.

Don't let this stuff get to you. After you've set up your system and gotten your memory configured, you can forget about all this stuff.

TIP

> If memory terms, memory expansion, and memory configuration all seem like synonyms for *major headache*, just get your local DOS wizard to help out. DOS weenies really thrive on memory configuration stuff—they think it's a major challenge to make every last byte of memory available for your programs.

Conventional Memory

The first part of your computer's memory is called *conventional memory*. This memory is also called lots of other things, such as *base memory*, *DOS memory*, or *that darned conventional memory*. Why the "darned" part? DOS (and therefore DOS programs) can only use 640K of memory, even though your computer might be equipped with more memory than that. When the first IBM PC was introduced, 640K seemed like a lot—it was ten times the amount of memory other computers had back then. Now it's barely enough for today's big, feature-filled programs. That's why 640K is also referred to as the "640K RAM Barrier."

You can find out how much conventional memory you have real quick with the CHKDSK command. (If you're using Windows, quit Windows by pressing Alt+F4 and then pressing Enter in Program Manager.) At the DOS prompt, type **CHKDSK** and press Enter. You see lots of stuff about your disk; bringing up the rear you see something like this:

```
655360 total bytes memory
613440 bytes free
```

"I HATE THIS!"

"It says I have 655,360 total bytes memory. Do I have 655K?"

Nope. You have 640K. 1K is 1,024 bytes. If you divide 655,360 by 1,024, you get 640. Generally, an approximation of your memory is fine; you don't need to divide every memory figure you see by 1,024.

Extended Memory

DOS and DOS programs are restricted to 640K of conventional memory. This limitation was built into DOS and into the design of the original IBM Personal Computer. But the need for more memory is an insistent drumbeat throughout history. Before long, programmers and users were clamoring for bigger programs that would require *megabytes* of RAM instead of just 640K.

The 640K RAM barrier is tough to break, just like the sound barrier used to be. But those clever engineers found two ways to get beyond it. The first, and by far the most important for you if you're using a 386 or newer computer, is *extended memory*, the subject of this section. The second, which is important only if you're using an older computer, is *expanded memory*. (Expanded memory is covered later in the chapter in the section, "What about Expanded Memory?")

Checklist

▼ *Extended memory*, also called XMS *memory*, is any memory beyond 1MB. (The memory between the 640K conventional memory and 1MB adds up to 384K, but it's different—it's called *upper memory*. Upper memory is discussed later.)

▼ Extended memory can be added only to computers that have the 80286, 80386, and 80486 microprocessors. (See Chapter 5 for an explanation of microprocessor model numbers.)

▼ If you have a 386 or 486, your system probably has *some* extended memory—probably 1MB of extended memory, for a total of 2MB, including conventional and upper memory.

▼ In general, DOS and DOS programs can't take advantage of extended memory. If you're just running DOS and DOS programs, you can have all the extended memory in the world, like 8MB, which will just sit there and not be used. A *few* applications, however, like Lotus 1-2-3 Release 3.X, can use extended memory.

▼ Extended memory comes into play when you use Microsoft Windows. Windows can use all the extended memory you can stuff into your computer.

Do You Have Extended Memory?

You can use the MEM command to find out if you are using DOS 5 or 6. Unlike CHKDSK (which only lists conventional memory), the MEM command lists all the types of memory you have in your system.

To use MEM, type **MEM** at the DOS prompt and press Enter. What you see on-screen depends on whether you have DOS 5 or DOS 6. Read on.

DOS 5 Memory Stats

With DOS 5, you see something like this (your screen will vary, depending on how the memory in your system is set up, how much memory is actually installed in your system, and the current location of the planet Jupiter in the zodiac):

```
 656384 bytes total conventional memory
 655360 bytes available to MS-DOS
 608640 largest executable program size


3145728 bytes total contiguous extended memory
      0 bytes available contiguous extended memory


1027072 bytes available XMS memory
```

For our purposes (figuring out how much extended memory you have, if any), the only thing worth noticing here is the "total contiguous extended memory" figure, four lines down in this example. This system has 3MB of extended memory.

"I HATE THIS!"

> ### "It says I have 3MB of extended memory but 0 bytes are available! Is my extended memory messed up?"
>
> It's OK. That "0 bytes available contiguous extended memory" line refers to an unused extended memory configuration technique. Just ignore this line. The one above it tells you how much extended memory is installed in your system.

DOS 6 Memory Stats

The DOS 6 MEM command produces output that's easy to understand:

I HATE PCs!

```
Memory Type          Total   =   Used   +   Free
- - - - - - - - - -           - - - - -     - - - - -     - - - - -
Conventional          640K       127K       513K
Upper                 155K        88K        67K
Adapter RAM/ROM       229K       229K         0K
Extended (XMS)       4096K      1944K      2152K


- - - - - - - - - -           - - - - -     - - - - -     - - - - -
Total memory         5120K      2388K      2732K
Total under 1 MB      795K       215K       580K
```

This command's output is pretty easy to read. This example shows a system with 4M of extended memory (XMS memory).

What about Expanded Memory?

The second way you can get around the 640K RAM barrier is called *expanded memory*, which is different from *extended memory*. (Don't get mad at me; I didn't make up these terms.)

Expanded memory is the only way to get beyond the 640K RAM barrier if you are using an older PC—one based on the 8088, 8086, or 80286 microprocessors. (Chapter 5 contains the gruesome details on microprocessors.)

▼ Unlike extended memory, expanded memory isn't added to the motherboard. It's added using one of those plug-in expansion boards that fit into the expansion slots inside your computer's case.

continues

▼ Expanded memory may be old-fashioned, but it's great for people who use DOS programs. Lots of DOS programs can use expanded memory. The expanded memory gives you room for larger documents, such as spreadsheets. Quattro Pro 4.0 is an example of a DOS application that can use expanded memory.

▼ Expanded memory is also called *EMS memory*.

And What Is This "Upper Memory Area" Thing?

Conventional memory goes from 0 to 640K. Extended memory goes from 1MB up. Well, what about the memory *between* 640K and 1MB? There's 384K of unaccounted space in there, and it's called *upper memory*. (It used to be called *reserved memory*.) In the original PC design, this area was set aside for various secret system purposes, but much of it isn't used. An unused portion of the upper memory is called an *upper memory block*. (UMB, pronounced like the *umb* in *numb*. Or *dumb*.)

One of the pet hobbies of DOS addicts is to move some DOS stuff into upper memory blocks. This leaves more room in conventional memory for your DOS programs, which is good. But it isn't something you should try doing yourself.

Yet Another Type of Memory

(High memory area)

There's *another* type of memory, believe it or not: the *high memory area* (*HMA*). You may run into this term now and then, if someone's trying

to ruin your day. Basically, the high memory area is the first 64K of extended memory. (Extended memory is the memory above 1MB, remember?)

OK, OK, I'll Look at the Map

To get a picture of the various kinds of memory, you might find it helpful to look at the following memory map. This system has 384K of conventional memory, 384K of upper memory, and 2MB of extended memory (which includes 64K of high memory area), for a total of 3MB. This diagram doesn't include expanded memory. Expanded memory is off by itself on an expansion board—it isn't part of the memory on the computer's motherboard.

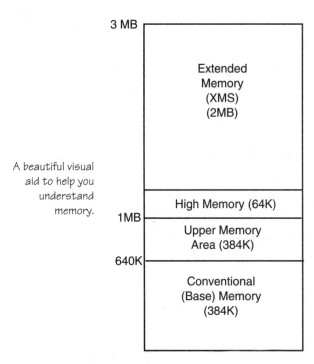

A beautiful visual aid to help you understand memory.

Top Ten Recent Discoveries of Computer Science

10. Computer actually invented by ancient Egyptians but given up, according to recently discovered hieroglyphics, because it was "obviously such a stupid idea"

9. Fans inside PC system units can be used to power model aircraft

8. Keystrokes on notebook computer can be picked up and recorded by neighbors using portable phones

7. Annual loss of 2% of GNP attributed to time wasted trying to learn distinction between *conventional memory* and *extended memory*

6. First personal computers invented by former Vietnam-era student radicals in underhanded plot "to bring capitalism to its knees"

5. Large, flat area of computer cabinet handy for stacking papers, disks

4. DOS originally designed to control large remote bulldozer at hazardous waste facility near Seattle

3. Increase in computer orders followed by similar upswing in aspirin, Tylenol sales

2. Wayne Newton is actually a computer-controlled robot begun as an experiment by IBM

1. Large, cumbersome, boring computer books perfect for propping up short table leg

Getting More Memory

(A great way to upgrade your system)

Thinking about upgrading your system? Probably the first thing you should do is add more memory. The best way to do this is to take your system to the store where you purchased it, or to a computer repair service, and have them do it for you.

Memory prices fluctuate according to market conditions, but you can usually get 1MB of RAM for about $75. Plan on spending another $50 or so for the installation. Shop around. In my area, one shop charged $150 per megabyte for a memory upgrade, including labor—another one charged just $80.

Even though you shouldn't attempt this upgrade yourself, you can speed the process (and make sure you're getting the right memory chips) by doing the following:

▼ Use CHKDSK or MEM to find out how much conventional memory you have. (These commands are discussed earlier in this chapter.) If you have less than 640K, say these magic words to the worker at the computer shop: "I want to bring my system up to 640K."

▼ Do you have a system based on the 8088, 8086, or 80286 processors? For DOS programs, your best bet is to add *expanded memory*. Make sure that the expanded memory conforms to the LIM 4.0 specification. This memory will come in the form of an expansion board that's pressed into those expansion slots inside your computer. There will be software, too, which will have to be installed. Have all this done for you.

CHAPTER 6

▼ Do you have a system based on a 386 or 486? If you have 2MB or less of extended memory, consider expanding to 4MB or 8MB. This memory will come in the form of *standard in-line memory modules* (SIMMs), each of which has 1MB of RAM. You need SIMMs that are fast enough for your computer. El cheapo SIMMs, rated at 80 ns (*ns* is short for *nanosecond*—one billionth of a second), may not be fast enough; you may need 70 ns chips. (The smaller the number, the faster.) Check your computer's manual or call the computer manufacturer to find the right speed.

Configuring Memory

If you check out the computer book section at the bookstore down at the mall, you'll find lots of books on configuring memory. To *configure memory* means to use *memory management programs* to set up your system's memory for your programs' use. The goal of memory configuration is to squeeze the last possible bit of space out of conventional memory and to make expanded or extended memory available for your applications.

BUZZWORDS

MEMORY MANAGEMENT PROGRAM

A program that helps you get the most out of your computer's memory. DOS comes with two memory management programs, called HIMEM and EMM386. You can also buy other memory-management programs. Their goals are to move some of DOS out of conventional memory into those nice, unused upper memory blocks or to HMA.

CHAPTER 7
Disks and Disk Drives

IN A NUTSHELL

▼ What disks are for
▼ The difference between floppy and hard disks
▼ How to tell which drive is drive A and which is drive C
▼ How to buy the right floppy disks for your system
▼ How to insert and remove floppy disks
▼ How to prevent the computer from changing the information on a disk
▼ How to format floppy disks

W hat are *disks*? Basically, they're the computer equivalent of the tape in a tape cassette. Just as a cassette recorder can play your cassette tape, the disk drive can *read* what's on your disk. Just as a cassette recorder can record on your cassette tape, the disk drive can *write* new information to the disk.

This chapter explains all the stuff you can do with disks.

What Disks Do

(Besides spin around in circles)

Take a look near anyone's computer, and you'll probably see disks all over the place. This is obviously one of the banes of computing—keeping all those darned disks organized. Why are they necessary? Three reasons:

▼ Your computer's memory (RAM) can't store stuff when the power's shut off. You need some place to store your programs and your work. Disks can do a very nice trick: hold the stuff that's on them without needing any electricity to do so.

▼ You will eventually have a lot more programs and work than your memory (RAM) can accommodate. That's why disks are necessary—they provide lots of storage space.

▼ You need some way to get new programs into your computer. When you buy programs, they come on disks. (To get them into your computer, you have to *install* them, as explained in Chapter 18.)

Floppy Disks vs. Hard Disks

Your system is probably equipped with one hard disk drive and one (or maybe two) floppy disk drives. A *disk drive* is the mechanism that makes the disk go around and access the information that's on it. The *disk* is the round thing.

A *floppy disk* is small (either 3.5 inches or 5.25 inches) and portable. You can take a floppy disk with you. The 5.25-inch disk is floppy (flexible). The 3.5-inch disk is covered with a hard plastic case, but it is still called a floppy disk, even though it's not floppy.

TIP

Of the two, bigger isn't necessarily better. 5.25-inch disks are vulnerable to damage because of a big, open area that lets the drive mechanism contact the surface of the disk. 3.5-inch disks have a cunning aluminum door that slides shut when you remove the disk from the drive. If you have a choice, use 3.5-inch floppy disks; they're more durable and they can store more information.

A *hard disk* is nonremovable; that is, you can't take it with you. You can't see the hard disk because it is inside the system unit (the big case that houses the CPU and the other stuff discussed in Chapter 5). A hard disk can store much, much more information than a floppy disk. And it's faster.

Which Drive Is Which?

Floppy drives look like mail slots on the front of your computer. If you have only one floppy drive, it's drive A. If you have two floppy drives, one is drive A, and the other is drive B. The first floppy drive in your system, probably the top one if you have two, is drive A and the bottom is drive B. Your hard disk is drive C.

"I HATE THIS!"

It says I have a drive F!

If you use a computer that's connected to a network, you see a *network drive*, which looks just like a hard disk from your viewpoint as you use DOS. It's probably called drive F, although the exact drive letter varies. If there are programs available on this "drive," you can run them as if they were installed on your computer. But take my advice: Get some help from the person who set up or maintains the network. Every network has its little peculiarities, and you'll need personal assistance to learn how to navigate the network correctly.

Buying the Right Floppies for Your System

Most computers now have a hard disk as standard equipment. Still, floppy disks have lots of uses. You can use them when you want to exchange files with someone, and you can also use them to make safe, backup copies of your work.

Sooner or later, you'll find yourself at the office supply or computer store, ready to buy some disks. You learn how in this section.

Floppy Disk Basics

You have to decode a lot of technical information in order to understand the different types of floppy disks. Here are the basics:

▼ These days, all computers come with double-sided (DS) drives, which can use both sides of the disk—much like you can use both sides of an audio tape. (Earlier computers used only one side of the disk.) The disks you buy still have the abbreviation DS on the box. Ignore the DS; it doesn't mean anything of value.

▼ Both kinds of disks, little and big, come in two storage capacities. (The next section reveals horribly fascinating statistics about capacities.)

▼ You can't use disks without formatting them. *Formatting* is a process in which the disk drive lays down a pattern on the disk's surface—a pattern that is needed for recording and reading data. This process is something like painting lines on a parking lot so that you know where to park cars. Formatting is covered later in this chapter.

Density and Capacity (Fraternal twins)

Not only do disks come in different sizes; they also come in different densities.

Density refers to the recording method (*how* DOS crams the information on a disk). There are two densities: double density and high density. Density is related to capacity—how much information can be stored on a disk. Double-density disks (DD) cannot store as much information as high-density disks (HD). On the positive side, double-density disks are cheaper.

CHAPTER 7

Capacity refers to the *amount* of data you can store and is measured in kilobytes or megabytes.

BYTE, KILOBYTE, and MEGABYTE

A *byte* equals about one typed character. A *kilobyte* (abbreviated K) equals around 1,000 bytes. A *megabyte* (abbreviated MB or M) equals around 1,000,000 bytes.

The Floppy Disk Match Up

Now that you know the different sizes and capacities, you have to match the right disk with the right drive. It's easy to figure out the size: you can't put a 5.25-inch disk in a 3.5-inch hole (unless you fold it, maybe).

It's more difficult to pick the right *capacity*. The trick is to determine the capacity of your drive. Remember that the drive has to be able to read the disk. The easiest way to find the capacity of your computer's disk drives is to ask someone at the store where you bought your computer. Or check the manuals that came with your system.

After you find out what kind of drive you have, use this table to figure out what disk you need:

You have this drive:	Buy these disks:
3.5-inch, 720K	3.5-inch DS, DD
3.5-inch 1.44MB	3.5-inch DS, HD

BUZZWORDS

You have this drive:	Buy these disks:
5.25-inch, 360K	5.25-inch, DS, DD
5.25-inch, 1.2MB	5.25-inch DS, HD

K=Kilobyte
MB=Megabyte
DS=Double sided (not important)
DD=Double density (stores less)
HD=High density (stores more)

TIP

An impressive trick known only to true computer geniuses
What's this disk? Is it double- or high-density? This question is pretty easy to answer for 3.5-inch disks because the manufacturers helpfully stamp HD on a corner of the disk. But what about 5.25-inch disks? Here's how to tell. Those old, obsolete double-density (360K) disks have a reinforcement ring about 1/8 inch wide around the hole in the center of the disk. The spiffy, new, modern 1.2MB disks don't.

Buying Disks

OK. You know what kind of disks you need. Now there are some tips on how to purchase disks:

▼ Buy formatted disks, if you can. You can format disks yourself, if you must, but this process is tedious; formatting a whole box of disks might take a half hour—maybe longer. Look for disks labeled *Formatted - IBM*. The IBM part refers to the IBM formatting standard; you can use these disks even if your computer wasn't made by IBM.

▼ You can save a little money by buying generic, no-name disks, but the disks might contain flaws. For reliable backups, choose disks from established, brand-name companies such as Verbatim, Memorex, 3M, or Maxell.

Inserting and Removing Floppy Disks

You've probably had some experience inserting and removing floppies already, so you know there's only one way you can look like a goof doing it: inserting it the wrong way. Here's the trick: Make sure the label is facing up and is toward you.

Then make sure that there isn't already a disk in the drive. Remove the disk before you insert another one.

Checklist

▼ If you're inserting a big (5.25-inch) disk, make sure that the drive door is unlatched. After you insert the disk, close the latch.

▼ If you're inserting a little (3.5-inch) disk, there's no latch. Just push the disk into the drive until it clicks into place. The drive button (which is just below the door) pops out when a disk is inserted.

▼ To remove a big (5.25-inch) disk, release the latch. The disk should pop out. If it doesn't, there's a space that lets you put two fingers in far enough to grab the disk.

▼ To remove a small (3.5-inch) disk, just press the button under the drive door. The disk pops out.

CAUTION

Don't force a disk into a drive. If it won't go in easily, there may be another disk in the drive, or you might be inserting the disk upside down or backward. Also, don't insert or remove disks when the little light is on. If you do, you could scramble the information on the disk.

Don't Mess with This Disk

Both kinds of floppy disks can be *write-protected*, which means you can prevent the computer from erasing what's on the disk or adding any new information to it. The computer can still read the information that's on the disk; it just can't alter the disk in any way. For this reason, you might want to write-protect a floppy disk that contains valuable data that you don't want to alter accidentally. Also, you should write-protect original program disks.

Checklist

▼ To write-protect a 5.25-inch disk, you use the little adhesive labels that come with the disks. Wrap the tab over the notch so that half of the tab covers the notch on one side and half of the tab covers the notch on the other side. To unprotect the drive, remove the label. If you used all the adhesive scraps to wrap Christmas presents, you can use Scotch tape instead.

▼ To write-protect a 3.5-inch disk, turn the disk over and find the little write-protect slider, which is on the upper left corner on the back of the disk. When you move it up to uncover the hole, the disk is write-protected. To unprotect the disk, move it down to cover up the hole again.

CHAPTER 7

"I HATE THIS!"

It says this disk is write-protected!

If you've write-protected a disk and try to save data on it, DOS gives you its "Write protect error" message. Just remove the disk, unprotect the disk, and try again.

Formatting Floppies

(The rite of initiation)

If you buy formatted floppy disks, you don't need to read this section. Lucky you! If you didn't buy formatted floppies, read on. This section explains the why and how of formatting.

Why format? A floppy drive can't use a disk unless it is formatted. *Formatting* is a disk version of boot camp—it makes sure the disk is ready to serve you with loyalty, honor, and courage. DOS makes the disk do lots of pushups and chin-ups and run 25 or so miles. You don't really need to understand everything that DOS does to the disk; you just need to know that this stuff must be done.

TIP

There's no visual difference between an unformatted and a formatted floppy disk. So that you can tell which ones you've formatted, put blank labels on the formatted ones. To be really sure about which ones are formatted, write a little "f" in the upper right corner of the label.

Formatting with DOS

You format a disk from the DOS prompt (C> or C:\>). Here's what you do:

1. Insert the unformatted disk into the drive.

2. Type the formatting command and press Enter.

If you're using drive A, type **FORMAT A:**.

If you're using drive B, type **FORMAT B:**.

CAUTION

> If you see the message, "WARNING: ALL DATA ON NON-REMOVABLE DISK DRIVE C WILL BE LOST", press N to cancel the operation! You're about to reformat your hard disk, which would cause endless grief. You should only format *floppy disks*, and those go in drive A or B. Don't ever, ever, ever type **FORMAT C:**. Ever.

3. You are asked to press Enter before proceeding. Make sure that you've inserted the correct disk in the drive, and that it doesn't contain any valuable data. Then press Enter. The format process begins!

At the conclusion of the format, you are prompted for a *volume label* (a fancy DOS term meaning *name*).

4. Type a volume label of up to 11 characters. This volume label will appear when you use the DIR command. If you are crazy about names, type one. Otherwise, just press Enter to skip the volume label.

After the format is complete, you see a message telling you how many bytes (characters) of storage are available on the disk. The message looks something like this:

```
1213952        bytes total disk space
1213952        bytes available on disk

512            bytes in each allocation unit
2371           allocation units available on disk

Volume Serial Number is 1D19-0FFD
```

5. After the message, you see a prompt informing you that you can format another disk. Press Y to format another one, or N to stop formatting and return to the DOS prompt. Then press Enter.

If you're using DOS 6, FORMAT checks to see whether the disk is already formatted. If so, FORMAT makes a backup copy of important information on the disk so that you can *unformat* the disk, should you later find that formatting the disk was a terrible mistake. (Say you happened to format a disk that contained information necessary to the known free world.)

CAUTION

Sooner or later, a "helpful" colleague will tell you that you can "save money" by buying double-density disks and then formatting them for high-density storage. Don't do it—the format won't be reliable.

Formatting with Windows

If you're using Microsoft Windows, you use File Manager to format your disks. File Manager is a program included with Windows that does the

same stuff DOS does—in a much more user-friendly manner. This is
how you format a disk using File Manager:

1. In Program Manager, choose Main from the Window menu. (To
do this, click on Window on the menu bar, and then click on Main
from the Window menu.)

2. In the Main program group, double-click on the File Manager icon.

3. Put the unformatted disk into the disk drive.

4. From the Disk menu, choose the Format Disk option.

5. From the Disk in list, click on the letter of the disk drive that contains the disk you're formatting.

6. If you are formatting a low-density disk, click on the down arrow
next to the Capacity box, and then choose the capacity of your
disk (360K for a 5.25-inch disk, or 720K for a 3.5-inch disk).

7. Click on OK or press Enter.

8. You see an alert box warning you that formatting will erase all the
data on the disk. Are you sure you want to proceed? If so, click on
Yes. If you're not sure, click on No.

9. When the disk is formatted, you see an alert box asking you
whether you'd like to format another disk. If so, click on Yes. If
not, click on No.

10. To exit File Manager and return to Program Manager, hold down
the Alt key and press F4.

Did Everything Go Smoothly?

Sometimes you run into problems while formatting disks. If you can't solve it, toss the disk into the trash—disks are cheap, but your time and data aren't.

You might see the error message `Track 0 is bad, disk unusable`. This message indicates that there's something wrong with the surface of the disk. But you also might get this message if you try to format a low-density disk using the high-density setting. Try again. If you still get the message, toss the disk.

If DOS or Windows reports that the disk has any "bad sectors," discard the disk.

Top Ten Uses for Dead Disks

10. Use as office Frisbee

9. Affix to coworker's hat to make zany Mickey Mouse ears

8. Insert into toaster just for the heck of it

7. Handy beer coasters

6. Hide in clothing and pretend disk contains Top Secret Government Information

5. Smart-looking saucers for office tea party

4. Pile up 3.5-inch disks to level legs of sofa, ottoman

3. Use as fuel for space-age Databurner fireplace insert

2. Spray-paint with snowflake stencil for festive holiday decorations

1. Target for popular Data Dart game

CHAPTER 8

Monitors
(Get the Picture?)

IN A NUTSHELL

▼ Why you need an adapter and a monitor to get a picture on-screen

▼ What all those acronyms mean

▼ What resolution is

▼ What size monitor you need

▼ Why you should or shouldn't get a color monitor

▼ How to protect yourself from electromagnetic radiation (EMR)

▼ How to adjust your monitor for optimum picture quality

▼ How to clean the screen, and why you'd better

▼ How to avoid the heartbreak of phosphor burn-in

Most of the time that you work with the computer finds you staring at that television thing—the monitor—except for those brief moments when you take a longing look at the Real World, which is passing you by as you work. What with your spending so much time at the monitor, the monitor had better be good. In this chapter, you learn what it takes to display a high-quality image on your monitor—and how to tell whether what you're seeing is the latest and greatest.

The Monitor and the Adapter

(It takes two)

Your computer requires two components to come up with a screen display: a monitor (the television-type thing) and a video adapter (an electrical thing housed inside the computer where you can't see it).

BUZZWORDS

> **VIDEO ADAPTER**
>
> Electronic stuff inside the computer that generates the screen display. There are lots of different video adapters, and they vary in quality. It's called an *adapter* because, in most computers, its circuitry is on one of those plug-in expansion boards that fits into one of the expansion slots in your system unit. (Some people call these *adapter boards*, just to confuse others.) In other computers, though, the video stuff is built into the motherboard.

▼ More than the monitor, the video adapter determines the quality of the text and graphics you see. Like your television, your monitor is just a *receiver*; something else has to be a *transmitter*. That's where the adapter steps in; it creates the signal that the monitor displays.

▼ If you want a better display, you probably need to upgrade your adapter *and* your monitor.

▼ Adapters fall into two general categories: color and monochrome (black and white).

▼ *Black and white* is a misnomer for early monochrome systems, which display green or amber characters on a black background. More recent monochrome systems display black text on a white background.

The Acronym-Collector's Guide to Computer Monitors

Your computer's video adapter creates the signal that is then conveyed, via a cable, to your monitor. The older ones don't do such a hot job of this. The newer ones do better: they show sharper text, handle graphics better, and offer hundreds of colors or gray shades. Among the computer community, all this knowledge is summed up in terse acronyms, like CGA and VGA, which you're just expected to know. If you don't, read on.

I HATE PCs!

CHAPTER 8

Fake Your Way to Video Adapter Knowledge

Adapter Type	Acronym	Faker's Guide
Color Graphics Adapter	CGA	The oldest color adapter, and pretty obsolete unless you only occasionally use the computer. Generates fuzzy text and just a few, garish colors. Not usually included with today's systems.
Monochrome Display Adapter	MDA	The oldest monochrome adapter. Great text quality, but one huge disadvantage: it can't display graphics. If you try to display a graph, for example, you just see a blank screen. Like the CGA, this adapter isn't often included with today's systems.
Hercules Graphics Adapter	HGA	Also called a *monographics adapter*, this adapter solved the MDA's no-graphics problem. Great text, good graphics. Often included in "budget" systems, and fine if you just want to use your computer for basic word processing and number crunching.

Adapter Type	Acronym	Faker's Guide
Enhanced Graphics Adapter	EGA	A much better color adapter than the CGA, this adapter produces great-looking text and graphics with lots of cool colors. But the VGA came soon afterward and offers even better performance for not much more money. You don't find too many systems with EGA adapters these days.
Video Graphics Array	VGA	The current "standard" adapter, which you find in almost all the 386SX budget systems being sold in places like Sears and K-Mart. Great text, lots of colors, and beautiful graphics. Good for both DOS and Microsoft Windows.
"Paper White" VGA		A monochrome VGA adapter that produces clear, sharp black text on a "paper white" background. People who produce black-and-white newsletters or brochures like this adapter because they can see on-screen how the final product will look.

continues

I HATE PCs!

CHAPTER 8

Fake Your Way to Video Adapter Knowledge, continued

Adapter Type	Acronym	Faker's Guide
"Gray Scale" VGA		This adapter is also monochrome, but it produces lots of intermediate gray shades that make pictures and drawings look really cool.
Super Video Graphics Array	SVGA	The sharpest and latest color VGA adapter, with even more colors. Awesome. The better computers sold today usually include an SVGA adapter.

Monitors Are Pretty Simple

(Compared to that awful adapter stuff)

The type of adapter you have generally determines what type of monitor you're using.

Checklist

▼ If you have a CGA adapter, you have a CGA monitor—also called an *RGB monitor*. RGB stands for "red, green, blue," the colors that make up the color display.

▼ If you have an MDA adapter, you have a monochrome monitor. The text looks great, but you don't get graphics. This is a pain when you're using a program such as Lotus 1-2-3 that allows you to see graphs that are automatically generated from the numbers you're crunching. But read on for a quick, cheap fix!

▼ MDA users, you can replace your MDA adapter with a "monographics" adapter (HGA) for very little money. Then you can see graphics on-screen without having to purchase a new monitor.

▼ If you have an HGA adapter, you have a "monographics" monitor. This is just fine if you're planning to run nothing but DOS programs like WordPerfect, but it won't work with Windows.

▼ If you have a VGA adapter, guess what? You have a VGA monitor. And it's probably color.

▼ If you have an SVGA adapter, you probably have a monitor designed to work with SVGA adapters. But you might have what's called a *multisynch* or *multiscanning* monitor, which automatically senses the type of signal your monitor is putting out and adjusts itself accordingly.

"I HATE THIS!"

Interlacing and dot pitch defined

Two characteristics of VGA and SVGA monitors affect their quality: whether interlacing is used, and the monitor's dot pitch specification.

Interlacing is a method of faking a high-quality display by "painting" half the screen in one cycle, and then doing the

"I HATE THIS!"

other half in the second cycle. This produces a faintly detectable screen flicker that can be fatiguing to the eyes. The best monitors are non-interlacing monitors; they don't use this trick. But they cost more.

The dot pitch measurement tells you how fine-grained an image a monitor can display. The smaller the measurement, the better. For example, .28mm (millimeters) is very good; .43mm isn't so hot.

What Is This "Resolution" Number All About?

When I said earlier that adapters have been getting "sharper" as time goes by, I was talking about *resolution*. And just what is resolution?

BUZZWORDS

RESOLUTION

Resolution is a measurement of the amount of detail your monitor can show. It is measured by the number of dots (called *pixels*) that can be displayed on each line, as well as the number of lines that can be displayed on each screen. (Why use an unfamiliar word such as pixels? Because the word dots doesn't sound nearly so impressive.)

▼ You'll see figures like 680 x 480 in advertisements and manuals. This figure means "680 dots per line and 480 lines per screen." 680 x 480 is the standard resolution for a VGA monitor, which is fine. SVGA resolutions are higher, such as 800 x 600 or 1,024 x 768.

▼ Your video adapter determines your monitor's display resolution. You can't improve the screen sharpness just by getting a better monitor; you have to get a better adapter, one that offers higher resolution.

Monitor Size

(Is bigger better?)

Adapters determine the overall quality of your computer's video display. But one thing the monitor determines is the size of the displayed image.

▼ The bigger the monitor, the better. You can see more of what you're working on, which makes it easier to keep track of what you're doing. And the characters are bigger, making the system easier on your eyes.

▼ A lot of systems come with 12- or 13-inch monitors, measured diagonally. 14-inch monitors are better—one or two little inches can make a huge difference.

continues

▼ You can even get 17-inch monitors, which are big enough to display two pages. These monitors are perfect if you're thinking of getting into *desktop publishing* (using your system to create and lay out newsletters, price lists, and other publications).

Monochrome or Color?

PC displays fall into two broad categories, monochrome (black and white or green and black or orange and black—two colors, basically) and color. Which is better? The short answer: color, although monochrome still has its advocates.

Why color?

▼ Color is worth having even if you're planning to do nothing but word processing (text only). Most programs use color to highlight menu options and display messages. A message displayed in a bright, garish yellow is a lot easier to see than one that blends with the text.

▼ Most programs designed today assume that you're using a color system. Of course, you can still run a lot of programs on a monochrome system, but they don't look as nice.

▼ If you think you'll *ever* run Windows, color is a must. Windows makes great use of color.

▼ Take a break and play a computer game. But to do so, you'll need a color display.

▼ For the most part, color does not improve DOS. You still see that colorless DOS prompt regardless of the type of monitor you are using.

▼ If you're using a monochrome adapter and display, do not despair. Many people feel that color is distracting and pointless, especially if you're using your computer for text processing. You print in black and white (mostly); why not see it in black and white?

EXPERTS ONLY

Will I glow in the dark after using my monitor?

Don't worry about X-rays, gamma rays, and all the rest of the really nasty stuff you may have heard about: today's computer monitors don't emit them in any measurable quantities. What may prove to be more dangerous to your health is a type of radiation that's emitted by just about every electrical device in homes and offices.

Many household devices, such as electric shavers, electric blankets, and computer monitors, emit extremely low-frequency (ELF) *electromagnetic radiation* (EMR). After years of denying that this radiation is dangerous, the scientific community is now coming up with some studies that suggest elevated rates of leukemia after prolonged exposure to such devices.

What about monitors? Most of the EMR emitted by computer monitors goes out the sides and the back of the monitor. And no matter which direction it goes, it falls off to undetectable levels at a distance of about 28 inches from the monitor.

I HATE PCs!

EXPERTS ONLY

To be ultra-safe, here are some tips:

▼ Work at least 28 inches from your monitor.

▼ Don't sit at a desk where you're close to the back or sides of someone else's computer.

▼ Those ever-cautious Scandinavians have worked out standards for EMR radiation. If you're really concerned about EMR, get yourself a low EMR radiation monitor that conforms to the Swedish standards.

▼ Don't waste money on a so-called radiation shield for your monitor. They don't block the type of EMR radiation that's been implicated in the health studies.

And What Adapter Do You Have?

Which video adapter is "under the hood" of the computer you're using? If you're using DOS 6, the MSD (Microsoft Diagnostics) program can tell you pronto. (If you don't have DOS 6, find out which adapter you have by asking the person who sold you the system or set it up for you.)

To find out which video adapter your system is using, type **MSD** and press Enter. You see a screen with a lot of big buttons. Just look next to the button labeled Video. You see the acronym of your adapter (like VGA or SVGA) followed by the manufacturer's name. If you really want to know more, press V or use your mouse to click on the Video button. You see a screen full of information, some of which is useful—such as whether your system is capable of color.

Press Enter to exit the Video dialog box, and then press F3 to quit MSD.

I HATE PCs!

What Are Those Funny Knobs?

Monitors usually have two knobs in addition to the On/Off switch. In keeping with the spirit of the PC, these knobs are usually carefully hidden. One knob controls brightness, the other controls contrast. Very few monitors actually label these knobs Brightness and Contrast. Most use incomprehensible symbols. A little experimentation, however, will reveal which is which.

TIP

The best way to adjust your monitor, wouldn't you know it, is to display good ol' DOS stuff. Do a DIR, and then adjust the brightness just to the point that the background remains dark. (If you go too far, you start to get a sickly hue in the background.) Then adjust the contrast just to the point where the letters start to get kind of fuzzy. That's it!

Cleaning the Screen

Computer monitors attract an unbelievable amount of dust, thanks to the static charge that accumulates on the glass surface. Keep some glass cleaner and paper towels handy—you'll need them frequently. But don't spray the glass cleaner directly on the glass; some of the liquid might seep into the monitor's innards. Instead, spray the glass cleaner on the paper towel, and then clean the glass.

CHAPTER 8

Top Ten Substances Found on Dirty Computer Screens

10. Miniscule pieces of potpourri from office mate who insists on decorating office in country theme

9. Orange film left from eating Cheetos too close to monitor

8. Spray globules of Pepsi from opening can too close to monitor

7. Smog fused with coworker's perfume (**Warning:** Possibly explosive)

6. Finger smutches

5. Eraser lint

4. Little white hairs from coworker's Angora sweater

3. Little brown hairs from coworker's pet Chihuahua

2. Dandruff

1. Rouge/talcum powder (tie)

The Heartbreak of Phosphor Burn-In

If you leave your monitor on for long periods, displaying the same thing all the while, the image can permanently impress itself onto the screen. Why? Doesn't matter. The point is that if you leave your monitor unattended for more than a few minutes, you should equip your system with a *screen saver program*. This program blanks your screen or uses moving pictures so that there is no set image on-screen if your computer receives no input after a set period—say, 5 or 10 minutes. Screen savers even

include sound to enhance the image. The current rage among Trekkies is a program called *Star Trek*, a screen saver that shows pictures of the Enterprise, Mr. Spock, and Captain Kirk. The $40 or so that it costs is well worth the price.

If you plan to run Windows, you don't need to go out and buy a screen saver program—one is built in. Unfortunately, it doesn't run with DOS or DOS programs.

TIP

If your screen goes blank, some helpful colleague has probably installed a screen blanking program on your computer. Just press a key or move the mouse to see your screen again.

EXPERTS ONLY

A graphics what?

Windows requires the graphics mode, which runs slowly. Consequently, a new market has emerged for *graphics accelerator boards*. These are plug-in adapter boards that replace your computer's present video adapter. They include all the necessary video adapter circuitry, but they also have a little processing chip that can really zip up your computer's video performance. But you only need a graphics accelerator board if you're running Windows, which runs notoriously slowly due to the complexity of its on-screen display.

CHAPTER 9

The Keyboard (And All Those Funny Keys)

IN A NUTSHELL

- ▼ Why the computer keyboard has more keys than a typewriter
- ▼ How to disarm toggle keys
- ▼ The purpose of all those arrow keys
- ▼ The purpose of all those keys with weird names
- ▼ What to do if you hear a beep while typing fast
- ▼ Rules of the keyboard
- ▼ How to avoid repetitive strain injuries while using the computer

I HATE PCs!

The computer is a genuine Space Age thing—sleek, incomprehensible, electronic. Why does it have a nineteenth-century keyboard? Because nobody has figured out any better way to get text into the computer.

Oh, sure, some computers are equipped to recognize a *few dozen* spoken words, but you'll have a lot more luck typing a letter into the keyboard than trying to dictate it to the computer. For now, computers have one trait in common with people: they talk better than they listen. So you're stuck with the keyboard for text input.

TIP

Keyboards vary considerably in quality. The cheap ones have a mushy feel and require a lot of effort to type. You're never quite sure whether you've pressed the key correctly. The good ones have just the right amount of "give," and click happily when you've finished the keystroke. If you're shopping for a computer, try the keyboard before you buy. And if you're stuck with a mushy keyboard, consider upgrading. It's an easy upgrade. You just plug the new one in and type away. Your computer will never even know the difference.

What the Keyboard Does

(Why all those funny keys?)

Your keyboard is used for two things: bossing around the computer (giving commands), and entering data. As you'll see, these two facts explain why it has a lot of extra, weird keys and that odd, calculator-style keypad full of numbers.

I HATE PCs!

CAUTION

Keep that keyboard plugged in. Your computer probably won't start—and might crash—if the cord's disconnected. Your keyboard plugs into the back panel of the computer in a round plug that has five little holes.

The standard, 101-key extended keyboard has lots of keys that you won't find on a typewriter. Why is it called *extended*? Because it has more keys than the old, 88-key non-extended keyboard, which hardly anyone uses anymore. The extended keyboard has four major regions: typewriter keys, function keys, cursor-movement keys, and the numeric keypad.

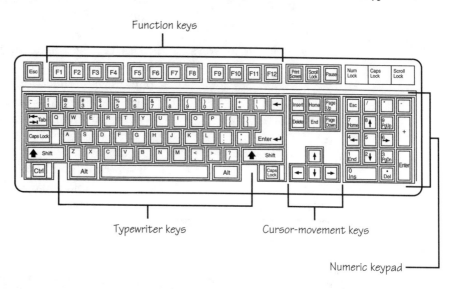

Function keys

Typewriter keys

Cursor-movement keys

Numeric keypad

Keys	The Scoop
Typewriter Keys	The "old" part of the keyboard is laid out just like a standard typewriter keyboard. You press Shift to create capital letters or those punctuation marks above the numbers.
Function Keys	These keys (F1, F2, F3, and so on) appear along the top of the typewriter keys. They do different things, depending on which program you're running. In most programs, for example, F1 is the Help key.
Cursor-Movement Keys	These keys let you move the on-screen *cursor*. (The *cursor* is the little blinking underline—or vertical bar—that shows you where your text will appear when you start typing.)
Numeric Keypad	If you know how to do the fingering for super-fast number entry, like they do at the bank, you can use the numeric keypad.

Top Ten Reasons to Use a Typewriter instead of a Computer

10. A lot cheaper

9. No nasty error messages, just that cute little ding!

8. Real writers do not use computers

7. Electricity optional

6. Combines keyboard, CPU, and printer in one compact, space-saving case

5. No agonizing decisions over which text typeface (font) to use

4. No software needed—load 8 1/2-by-11-inch paper for word processing, index cards for database management, and so on

3. Less clutter: no disks, no manuals, no nerds

2. You only have to learn a couple of terms, like *platen* and *carriage*

1. Tap-tap-tap clatter has promising potential to drive coworkers nuts

Those Highly Irritating Toggle Keys

The word *toggle* is highly familiar to anyone who spent his or her child-hood building model railroads, ham radios, or those Lego structures. For the rest of us, toggle doesn't mean a whole lot—there's only the sugges-tive fact that it rhymes with *boggle*. Here's a tip: the word basically means *switch*. When you toggle something, you switch it on or off.

The first time you press a toggle key, you turn on whatever it does. On most keyboards, a helpful little light comes on to let you know that you've engaged the key. The second time you press it, you turn it off. And right in synch, the light goes off.

Your keyboard has three toggle switches: Caps Lock, Num Lock, and Scroll Lock. Note them and beware. If you press them, the keyboard may do unexpected, funny things.

CHAPTER 9

TIP

> If your computer starts doing funny things, check the keyboard to see whether you've accidentally pressed one of the toggle keys.

That Cranky Caps Lock Key

By far the most irritating toggle key is the Caps Lock key. When you press it, you get uppercase letters, like on a typewriter. That's not so weird. What's weird is what happens when Caps Lock is on and you use the Shift key while you are typing. You get lowercase letters! lIKE tHIS. vERY iRRITATING. Of course you only notice this after typing half a page of text. Also irritating: Caps Lock shifts only the letter keys, not the numbers. This differs from the way a typewriter works.

The Numskull Num Lock Key

Very nearly as irritating is the Num Lock key, which controls the way the numeric keypad operates. When Num Lock is on, you get numbers when you press the number keys. When Num Lock is off, you can use the numeric keypad to move the cursor. So what's so bad about that? Unlike the other toggle keys, Num Lock is set up on most computers so that it's on when the computer starts. I like to use the numeric keypad to move the cursor, but I get 442886667 instead. Horribly unsavory.

The Innocent Scroll Lock Key

In contrast to its two pesky counterparts, Scroll Lock isn't a troublemaker. In fact, it doesn't do much of anything these days. The key actually does something interesting when you're running a spreadsheet program, but otherwise it doesn't do much more than turn the Scroll Lock light on or off.

Decoding All Those Keys with Arrows on Them

Some keyboards helpfully put the words Tab and Enter on the so-named keys, along with arrows. Some keyboards have only the arrows. Here's how to decode what the keys mean:

Key	Name	The Scoop
←	Backspace	You press this key to rub out the character to the left of the cursor. It's a pretty neat key because it lets you correct mistakes right after you make them.
↵	Enter	In DOS, you press Enter to send a command to the computer.
⊢← →⊣	Tab	This key doesn't do much in DOS, but it works a lot like its typewriter counterpart in word processing programs.
→	Right arrow	This cursor-movement key moves the cursor right one character.
←	Left arrow	This key moves the cursor left one character.
↓	Down arrow	This key moves the cursor down one line.
↑	Up arrow	This key moves the cursor up one line.

"I HATE THIS!"

The cursor won't move!

Don't bother trying to move the cursor if you're working with DOS (you see the C:\> prompt). You can't use the arrow keys to move the cursor with DOS. You can with most programs, though.

Hey! This Isn't a Typewriter!

In addition to the arrow keys, you'll notice some other unfamiliar keys on the keyboard. Nope, you're definitely not using a typewriter anymore.

Key	The Scoop
Esc	This Escape key generally cancels the current operation or takes you back to what you were doing previously.
Del or Delete	When you press this key in most programs, it erases the character that the cursor is on or the character to the right of the cursor.
Ctrl	Some programs use this key with another key to select a command. For instance, you might press Ctrl and B to select the Bold command.
Alt	You use this key, like the Ctrl key, for commands. It works the same way the Ctrl key does; you hold it down and press another key.

Key ·	The Scoop
Ins or Insert	For the most part, this key turns on a program's Insert mode, which lets you insert characters within text you've already typed instead of typing over the text. In a lot of programs, the cursor changes from a thin little underline to a big fat block after you switch to the Insert mode.
Home	Programs usually use this key to move the cursor to the beginning of a line or the beginning of a document. Sometimes, however, this moves the cursor to the first on-screen character.
End	Programs usually use this key to move the cursor to the end of a line or the end of a document. Sometimes, however, this key moves the cursor to the last on-screen character.
PgUp	Programs usually use this key to scroll the screen up toward the beginning of your file.
PgDn	Programs usually use this key to scroll the screen down toward the end of your file.
Prt Scr or Print Screen	Use the this key to get a quick printout of what's on-screen. Don't expect great quality, though. Use your program's Print command to print your work.

continues

Key	The Scoop
Pause/Break	You can press this key to stop a DOS command such as DIR from scrolling. When used in combination with the Ctrl key, this key cancels a DOS command.
\	This is the backslash key. It's used a lot in DOS to indicate subdirectories.
/	This is the forward slash key. It's used in spreadsheet programs such as Lotus 1-2-3 to display the Command menu. In mathematical expressions that you sometimes type, it means *divide*. 4/2 means, "4 divided by 2."

"I HATE THIS!"

It tells me to type Ctrl+A, but I can't get it to work!

Computer manuals use expressions like "Ctrl+A" to indicate a key combination. Key combinations work like this: you hold down the first key (Ctrl in this case), and then press the second key (A in this case—either uppercase or lowercase). You don't actually type the plus sign. If you see an expression like "F10, M," it means, "Press F10 and release the key. Then press M." (**Note:** Sometimes, key combinations are indicated with a hyphen rather than a plus sign, like this: Ctrl-A. The hyphen means the same thing as the plus sign. Ctrl-A is the same thing as Ctrl+A.)

What to Do If You Hear a Beep while Typing Really Fast

The quick, easy answer: slow down and let the computer catch up.

There is, of course, a boring technical explanation. Sometimes programs have to stop accepting keyboard input because they're busy doing something else, like saving your data to disk. You can keep typing for a little while, thanks to something called the *type-ahead buffer*, a temporary storage area that can store keystrokes while your computer is busy. But as soon as the type-ahead buffer is full, you hear a beep, which warns you that the characters you're typing at the moment will be lost. Wait until the program has finished doing what it's doing, and then resume typing.

Most programs can handle keyboard input as fast as you can dish it out.

TIP

Do you have to type the same character twice? Just hold down the key; most keys on the keyboard—even the cursor-movement keys—repeat when you hold them down. Try it. There's a delay, and then the repeat kicks in at a pretty fast rate.

Keyboard Styles of the Rich and Famous

The computer elite follow a set of handy, try-this-first rules, which naturally are never explicitly given to beginners.

I HATE PCs!

▼ Never indent by pressing the space bar. The text might not look aligned when printed, even if it looks right on-screen. Always use the Tab key to indent text.

▼ When typing text, only press Enter when you want to start a new paragraph. Most programs use a thing called *word wrapping*, which makes it unnecessary for you to press Enter when you reach the right margin. In word wrapping, the program automatically detects when a word would go over the margin, and *wraps* (moves) it down to the beginning of the next line. If you make changes in the paragraph, the program automatically adjusts the line wrapping for you.

▼ In many DOS programs, and in all Windows applications, pressing Alt or F10 activates the menu bar, the bar across the top of the screen that lists menu names. After activating the bar, you can press the highlighted or underlined letter to "pull down" a menu.

▼ Esc is the universal get-me-out-of-this command. You can use Esc to cancel a menu or on-screen dialog box, if you've decided against choosing an option.

▼ In Windows and most DOS applications, pressing F1 gets you on-screen help.

▼ In DOS, use Ctrl+C or Ctrl+Break to cancel a command that's not working out right. If you've just used DIR to display a directory and it's scrolling by too fast, press Pause to stop the scrolling. Then press any key to continue.

▼ Don't try to attack key combinations by crashing down on them at the same time. Hold down the Alt or Ctrl key, and then type the second key in the combination.

▼ Sometimes you'll see the message, `Press any key when ready (or to continue)`. This isn't exactly true: you can press any key, except Shift, Ctrl, Alt, Num Lock, or the 5 key on the numeric keypad.

▼ Some programs make extensive use of key combinations that might involve three or more keys—kind of a computerized version of Twister. For example, you may be told to press Shift+Ctrl+Q. This means, "Hold down the Shift and Ctrl keys, and while both of them are being held down, press Q."

▼ A lot of programs come with a thing called a *keyboard template*. This is an adhesive "cheat sheet" that fits on your keyboard. You can use the template to remember frequently used keyboard commands that you keep forgetting. If you use one program most of the time, stick its template to your keyboard.

CAUTION

Ctrl+Alt+Del reboots your computer, but it's dangerous—it wipes out everything in the computer's memory. If some of that stuff includes unsaved work, it's G - O - N - E, forever, period. Press Ctrl+Alt+Del only if you're sure your computer has crashed. A pretty good way to tell: nothing is happening on-screen, and when you try to type, you just hear beeps— even after 5 or 10 minutes.

What's That Funny Numb Feeling?

As rhythm guitarists have known for a long time, repeating the same hand action over and over and over can lead to health problems, which doctors call *repetitive strain injury* (RSI). This condition can cause a

really painful nerve disorder when scar tissue builds up in narrow areas of the hand and wrist. RSI can be serious and debilitating. A symptom of the injury is numbness in your fingers.

You can reduce your chances of contracting a repetitive strain injury by using the keyboard correctly.

Checklist

▼ Don't use a keyboard that's way up on the top of the desk. It should be positioned so that you can type with your elbows forming a right angle, and that usually means lowering the keyboard. If necessary, get a keyboard shelf that fits under your desk and slides out as needed.

▼ Be sure to rest your palms on something while typing. You can purchase a pad from your local computer store for this purpose.

TIP

IBM PC Books distributes AccessDOS, a program developed by the University of Wisconsin, for a nominal fee (call 800/426-7282). This program allows for single-fingered typing of key combinations, ignores accidental keystrokes, adjusts the key repeat rate, provides visual cues in place of the computer's beep, and includes extensive help screens. Alternative keyboard layouts for single-handed users are also available. For more information on products and services for people with disabilities, call the University of Wisconsin's Trace R & D Center, at 608/263-2309.

CHAPTER 10

Printers
(The Myth of the Paperless Office)

IN A NUTSHELL

▼ What kind of printers are available, and how they differ

▼ What serial and parallel printers are

▼ Printer names

▼ How to get someone else to hook up your printer

▼ What fonts are, and how you can get more of them

▼ How to see whether your printer is working

▼ Why you shouldn't bother printing from DOS

▼ How to deal with common printing problems

I HATE PCs!

A few years ago, geniuses at a major West Coast think tank predicted that the use of paper would soon disappear completely. We'd be working in "paperless offices," reading everything on computer screens. The atmosphere in the board rooms of paper companies was very gloomy. Hunched over, with their heads in their hands, the directors said things like, "We're doomed."

But it wasn't to be. Instead of giving up on paper, computer users have led the biggest paper-gobbling boom in history. Much to their surprise, paper company people watched profits and stock prices zoom upward. Today, the "paperless office" idea is dismissed as a joke.

Part of the reason is that just about every computer application program is designed to help you print stuff on paper. Word processing programs, for example, take the place of typewriters, while spreadsheet programs take the place of those vertically lined sheets that accountants and bookkeepers use. Maybe we'll use computers differently in the future, but for now, getting it down on paper is what completes the job.

The weak link in the whole chain is the printer, which all too often is an unwilling accomplice. It won't respond, the paper gets jammed, it runs out of paper—there's a whole string of annoyances that these devices are all too ready to spring on the unsuspecting user. This chapter surveys the world of printers, and tells you what to do when one of these annoyances comes up.

Types of Printers

Engineering geniuses the world over have invented dozens of ways to print computer output, but you'll find only four kinds of printers in widespread use today.

The Printer	The Scoop
Dot-Matrix Printers	The cheapest printers, these work by hammering a pattern (or *matrix*) of little wires against a ribbon, making an impression on paper. These printers tend to be noisy, and sometimes the dots don't connect very well. The best ones produce OK output, but they're slow because they have to go back over the printed text two or three times to connect all the little dots.
Inkjet Printers	These printers are more expensive than dot-matrix printers, but less expensive than laser printers. They work by spraying the paper with ink. The output looks something like the print created by a laser printer. Inkjet printers are slower than most laser printers.
Laser and LED Printers	These printers use parts from copying machines and work like copying machines, except that the image comes directly from the computer. Print quality is very good, and they print quickly (the best ones can print eight or more pages per minute of double-spaced, plain text).

continues

The Printer	The Scoop
PostScript Laser Printers	These printers are much more expensive than any other type of printer because they have their own built-in computer. The computer is needed to interpret printing instructions given in the printer's language (called *PostScript*). PostScript is needed only if you're doing professional desktop publishing.

You can also get color printers these days, and the quality of the output keeps improving. But these printers are still much more expensive to buy than one-color printers, and some of them require special, expensive paper.

Serial and Parallel Printers

Many printers are available in two models, serial and parallel. A *serial printer* is designed to be hooked up through one of your computer's serial ports. A *parallel printer* is designed to be hooked up through one of your computer's parallel ports.

BUZZWORDS

PORT

A *port* is a connection in the back of your computer that lets you hook up accessories like printers and modems.

I HATE PCs!

CHAPTER 10

Hooking up a printer to a parallel port is easy. You just connect the cables. Because it's such a hassle to connect printers through the serial port, most of today's printers are parallel printers.

If you're using a system that's already set up and is working fine, don't worry whether it has a serial printer. Someone has made the system modifications that are necessary to get the darned thing to work.

Printer Names

(Besides "#$%&!")

Your computer is designed so that it can be hooked to three or four printers. Because you're probably just hooking up one printer, the whole process should be uncomplicated, no? Well, of course not. After all, DOS is involved.

To give you the ability to use more than one printer, DOS has a set of printer names, such as LPT1:, LPT2:, COM1:, COM2:, and so on. (The colons are part of the name; they make the names easy to misspell.) The LPT ports are *parallel ports*, while the COM ports are *serial ports*. Chances are that your computer has just one parallel port, and if so, it's LPT1:.

If you need to hook up a printer to a parallel port and if you have the right cable, all you do is connect the cables. See the next section, "Making the Physical Connection."

If you have a serial port, read the section "Connecting a Serial Printer."

Checklist

▼ If you've just bought a computer, don't take it out of the salesroom until the salesperson shows you which of those funny-looking plug-holes is LPT1:.

▼ DOS, as well as your programs, assumes by default that you're using LPT1: to connect your printer. Moral of the story: your life will be much easier if you connect your printer to LPT1:. You won't be able to use a printer connected in the other ports unless you make modifications to your programs or to DOS.

Making the Physical Connection

To connect your printer, you need a *printer cable*. Finding the right printer cable should be a snap, but it isn't—thanks to a lack of printer cable standards. There are lots of different kinds of connectors, and to top it off, you have to know the *sex* of the connectors (male or female). Obviously, this is a very distasteful and embarrassing subject, one that is best left to the salespeople at the store where you bought the computer. Just say, "I want a cable to connect my printer," and take the one that is given to you. Be sure to ask where you need to plug in the cable because some computers have two plugs that look exactly the same. And if the cable doesn't work, take it back, make a bit of a fuss, and force the sales-person to give you the right cable.

Connecting a Serial Printer

(You've been warned)

Don't try to hook up a serial printer! There are several reasons why serial printers are hard to hook up. (If you have to hook up a serial printer, get someone who thrives on technical challenges to help you.)

Checklist

▼ You need the right cable. There are lots of different serial cables for different purposes. Getting the right cable for your serial printer can be something of a trick. Unfortunately, many computer salespeople are not knowledgeable about this matter and don't know which cable to give you.

▼ You have to connect the cable to the right COM port. Chances are, your computer has only one parallel port, but has two (or more) serial ports. Try to get the salespeople or technical support people to show you which COM port is which, among all those odd plug-in doohickeys on the back of your computer.

▼ You have to *configure* the serial port to meet your printer's characteristics. You do this by using a DOS command called MODE. If you don't type this command at the beginning of every session, your printer won't work.

▼ Just which MODE command you should type depends on your printer's needs, so check your printer's manual. If you are setting up your printer for the COM1: port, the command would look something like this:

    MODE COM1:9600,N,8,1

continues

155

I HATE PCs!

▼ If you're setting up the printer for the COM2: port, it would look something like this:

MODE COM2:9600,N,8,1

▼ The exact stuff you're supposed to type in the 9600,N,8,1 area varies from printer to printer. Good luck! Have fun!

The Joy and Anguish of Printer Fonts

Today's printers usually come with two or more built-in fonts—that is, complete sets of letters and numbers in a distinctive typeface design. These designs have creative names that don't tell you a lot about them; you're just supposed to know what the fonts look like. Here are some examples:

Bodoni

New Century Schoolbook

Avant Garde

Helvetica

Times Roman

Garamond Condensed

Courier

Checklist

▼ Some fonts come in alternative versions, such as Utopia Light or Helvetica Narrow.

▼ Every printer has a default font, the one that it uses unless some clever program tells it otherwise. DOS isn't clever, so it always prints with the default font.

▼ Most laser printers proudly offer Courier as the default font. Courier is amazing: using a thousand-dollar computer printer, it produces output that looks as though it were typed on a $98 typewriter.

▼ Usually, laser printers come with at least four or five built-in fonts.

▼ With many printers, you can add additional fonts by using *font cartridges*. To use these fonts, you simply plug the cartridge into the printer's cartridge slot.

▼ If your printer has a lot of memory, it might be able to use soft fonts. *Soft fonts* are stored on your computer's hard disk until needed, at which time they are sent (the term is *downloaded*) to your printer. Good word processing programs, such as WordPerfect, handle soft fonts automatically.

▼ To use your printer's fonts, your programs must be compatible with your printer. For more information on this bad news, read the section called "Program to Printer," near the end of this chapter.

▼ You can choose font sizes as well as fonts. Font sizes are measured in printer's points (72 per inch). The standard size is 12 points, which gives six lines per inch—the same as an office typewriter.

continues

Checklist, continued

▼ If you're using DOS applications, don't expect to see your font and font size choices on-screen. You just sort of have to imagine how they'll look. A few programs (such as WordPerfect) give you print preview modes that let you see how the document will look when printed.

▼ With Windows, you can use TrueType fonts. These are soft fonts especially designed to work with Windows. You see the fonts on-screen as well as in your printed documents. If you're using TrueType fonts, you often can print the fonts without having to purchase cartridges or any other accessories.

Top Ten Rejected Font Names

10. IRS Tax Form Gothic

9. Bud Light

8. USDA "Choice" Block Letter Bold

7. Graffiti Dingbats

6. Yellow-Pages Lawyer Fine Print Narrow

5. Gang Territory SprayPaint Italic (outdoor use only; large-caliber automatic weapon strongly suggested)

4. Madonna

3. Publisher's Clearinghouse FormLetter Ultra (large font sizes only)

2. Ayatollah Calligraphic Death Threat Condensed (requires hostage)

1. NewEnquirer Roman (requires third-grade education only)

Test Your Printer

(And your ability to withstand stress)

To test whether your printer works, make sure that the power's on and the printer is loaded with paper.

To print, your printer must be *on line* or *selected* (ready to receive stuff from the computer). This is usually the case, but check to make sure. Look for a button called On Line or Select. This button probably has an indicator light. When it's on, the printer is ready to go. (If it's off, press the button to turn on the light.)

"I HATE THIS!"

On line, off line, out of line

Why would someone have turned off the On Line button? With most printers, you have to take the computer *off line* (a techie expression that means "break the connection") to advance the paper. Most printers have Line Feed and Form Feed buttons that advance the paper one line or one page at a time, respectively. If the printer's off line, someone probably wanted to eject a page.

When your printer is on and selected, type **DIR > PRN** at the DOS prompt and press Enter. This command tells DOS to send the command's output to the printer. This command prints the current directory.

(If you're using Windows, you have to click the MS-DOS Prompt icon in the Main program group to display the DOS prompt. Then you can use this command. When you're finished using DOS, type **EXIT** and press Enter to return to Windows.)

"I HATE THIS!"

It won't respond!

Is the printer on? Is the printer selected (on line)? Is there a cable between the printer and the computer? Did you type the command correctly? Is there paper in the printer? Is there a user at the keyboard? Is the user reading a Harlequin romance again instead of typing these wonderfully cool DOS commands?

If you've checked all the obvious stuff and your printer still doesn't work, don't torture yourself. Find someone who knows this system, and get help. That's especially true if you're using a printer that's on a network. Almost always, you have to do something unusual to get network printers to respond.

Program to Printer

(Can you hear me?)

Your programs *talk* (electronically, that is) to your printer. Why do your programs have to talk to your printer? To get your printer to do fancy stuff, like printing bold or italic. Your program has to send a command

(an instruction) to the printer to turn on these special features, and then send another command to turn them off when they're no longer needed. The command set for a particular printer is called a *printer control language*. And when the printer and the program can converse, they are said to be *compatible*.

▼ Each printer brand has its own pet language. Commands written for one printer's language will do weird, unpredictable things if sent to another manufacturer's printer.

▼ Because of the post-Tower of Babel situation among printer manufacturers, software publishers must keep abreast of all the popular printers, and they must include special files, called *printer drivers*, with DOS programs. When you're buying a DOS program, make sure it has a printer driver for your printer. If it doesn't, you may not be able to use many of your printer's features.

▼ If your printer is compatible with your programs, life will be easy. You'll be able to print without too much hassle, and you'll be able to take advantage of all your printer's features. If the printer is not compatible, contact the software company, which might have a special supplementary disk containing a driver that will work with your printer.

▼ Windows programs don't need printer drivers. That's because Windows handles all this printer driver business itself. If Windows has a driver for your printer, you're in business; any Windows application will print with your printer.

▼ One way to make sure that your printer is compatible is to go with the herd: use a printer that just about everyone else is using. That means sticking with name brands, such as Hewlett-Packard or Epson. Hewlett-Packard is abbreviated HP.

continues

Checklist, continued

▼ A lot of printers are capable of *emulating* popular printers, such as HP printers. If your printer is said to have "HP emulation" or "Epson emulation," it will probably work with just about any program.

BUZZWORDS

PRINTER DRIVER

A *printer driver* is a file that tells the program how to use a particular brand of printer, such as the Keen-O-Matic XL1568. Part of installing a program is telling it which printer you're using so that the installation utility can go fetch the correct printer driver.

So what's a *compatible printer?* It's a printer your program supports. By that, I mean that your program has a printer driver for the particular make and model of printer you're using.

The Pain and Heartbreak of Printing Problems

When you are printing, lots of things can go wrong. Most of them aren't serious.

▼ The printer might not respond. Check to see whether the On Line or Select light is on. If it's not, push the On Line or Select button.

▼ The paper can jam. If you are using a laser printer, you may have to open the cabinet and extricate the jammed pages from various rollers, clamps, and other sadistic devices. Be careful! One of those rollers is really hot.

▼ Your printer can run out of paper. If so, your program will probably display a message informing you of this development. Load some more.

▼ If you have a laser printer, loading paper is easy. Just refill the tray. Loading paper is a feat unto itself with a dot-matrix printer. Sometimes you have to weave and bob and weave and clamp the paper through the printer. Ask someone to help you.

▼ You might see funny-looking garbage on your printout. If you're trying to print with DOS, this is pretty normal. If you're trying to print with a program, though, something's wrong. Maybe the program isn't set up for the printer you're using. Get someone who knows the program to help you. As a last resort, read the manual.

CHAPTER 11

Accessories
(Stuff to Max out Your Credit Card)

IN A NUTSHELL

▼ Mice, trackballs, graphics tablets, and
joysticks

▼ Surge protectors

▼ Uninterruptable power supplies

▼ Tape backup drives

▼ Sound boards

▼ CD-ROM drives and disks

▼ Additional, fascinating
gadgets

Y ou can equip your basic, humdrum PC system with lots of hardware accessories that can make this otherwise boring system do neat things. For example, imagine having a 21-volume encyclopedia available on-screen while you're working on a report. Or imagine hearing the main theme from Beethoven's Ninth in full digital stereo while seeing the score on-screen. And the next time you try Flight Simulator, imagine having an aircraft-style stick instead of having to get out of the Red Baron's way by pecking at the arrow keys.

The hardware accessories that make such wonders possible are called *peripherals*, a category that includes printers (discussed in the previous chapter), as well as modems and fax boards (discussed in the next chapter). A peripheral is any hardware accessory that isn't part of a very basic PC system.

Some of the peripherals discussed here, such as a mouse, might be included in your system already. Other peripherals, such as surge protectors, *should* be included in your system. Still others are great additions, especially if you want to use your computer for certain specific purposes, such as desktop publishing (creating cool-looking documents like newsletters completely on the computer) or helping to educate your kids. And some, like joysticks, really don't have any good justification but are awfully fun to have. So call the bank, find out how much room is left on your Visa, and let's get going.

Of Mice and Men

Most computers now come equipped with a mouse, that little soap-sized thing that sits on the table next to the keyboard. Inside the mouse is a ball that spins when you move the mouse around on the table top. As you move the mouse, a pointer (it usually looks like an arrow) moves around on-screen. You can perform tasks easily—like choosing commands—by moving the pointer to an on-screen object (such as an item in a list) and clicking the left mouse button.

I HATE PCs!

▼ In most programs, you can use a mouse to move the cursor really fast—just point to where you want the cursor to be, and click the button. No fussing with those arrow keys.

▼ When you choose commands by using the mouse, you cut down on keyboard fussing. If your application has a *menu bar*—a bar across the screen with names of commands—you can just point to a command and click to display the command menu. To choose an option, such as Print or Save, just click the option name.

▼ You can use Windows without a mouse, but lots of cool Windows features are designed with the mouse in mind.

▼ A mouse is crucial if you intend to use any drawing packages.

▼ A mouse is also really handy for selecting text for editing and formatting.

▼ The mouse isn't as useful if you're only using DOS programs—rather than Windows programs—but how useful a mouse is in DOS programs varies. Some programs (like dBASE IV Version 1.1) don't recognize a mouse at all, even if one is connected to your system. (The newest version of dBASE does include mouse support.) Others, like WordPerfect, support the mouse sort of indifferently, as if the software publisher wasn't really convinced people would want to use the thing. Still others, such as Microsoft Word for DOS, use the mouse in much the same, neat way that Windows does.

Who doesn't like the mouse? Some people who are expert touch-typists dislike having to take their fingers away from the keyboard. If you agree, you can ignore the mouse; most programs, including Windows programs, include keyboard equivalents for most mouse procedures.

TIP

Remember that almost all mouse maneuvers require the left mouse button. Only a few, oddball commands require the right button. If your mouse has three buttons, it's a safe bet that the middle one's about as useful as a hood ornament on a '56 Chevy.

"I HATE THIS!"

It says I'm not using the right mouse software!

To use your mouse, you or someone else must install the mouse software on your hard disk. Programs sometimes require you to use the latest version of this software. If you're using a Microsoft mouse, you automatically get the latest mouse software when you upgrade to the latest version of DOS. If you're using a non-Microsoft mouse, write to the company that makes the mouse and ask for the latest version of the mouse software. Hope they're still in business!

Types of Mice

Mice come in two varieties: serial and bus (in case you are curious). A *serial mouse* plugs into one of your computer's serial ports, or into its special, round mouse port (if it has one). A *bus mouse* plugs into an expansion board, one of those things that's pressed into the slots inside your computer's case.

If you already have the mouse and it's working fine, you probably don't need to fret over what kind you have. If you want to add a mouse, keep in mind that a serial mouse is a lot easier to hook up, and it's the one to choose if your computer has a special mouse port. If your computer lacks such a port and your serial ports are all taken up with other things, you can get a bus mouse. Get your local computer wizard to install it for you.

Using a Mouse

A mouse is pretty easy to use, once you've mastered the basic techniques of pointing, clicking, and dragging. Still, Windows users quickly discover that you need to devote some thought to keeping the little rodent happy.

Checklist

▼ Don't let the cord get tangled up in stuff. You won't be able to move the mouse freely, which is pretty frustrating.

▼ Keep an area clear for the mouse's use. You need about one square foot.

▼ If you run out of room to complete a mouse maneuver, you can pick up the mouse, reposition it on the desktop, and complete the maneuver.

▼ Some programs, including Windows, let you adjust mouse characteristics such as how fast the mouse pointer moves as you move the mouse. Lefties can swap the buttons so that the most frequently-used button is right under their index finger. To adjust the mouse with Windows, double-click on Control Panel in the Main program group, and then double-click on Mouse. You see lots of things you can change. Make your changes, and then click on OK to confirm your changes.

▼ If your desk has a smooth top and the mouse ball doesn't seem to find its footing, get a mouse pad. This provides just the right "feel" for the ball.

continues

▼ About once every two weeks (longer if you don't use your computer much), remove the mouse ball and clean it. Use Windex and a paper towel.

▼ Windex is also pretty good for getting potato chip grease off the mouse case.

"I HATE THIS!"

There's no pointer!

If you're using DOS at the DOS prompt, don't despair: DOS doesn't use the mouse. Look for the pointer again after starting your application. If you still don't see it, get your local computer zombie to install the mouse software for you.

Trackballs

Some computers are equipped with a *trackball*, which is like an upside-down mouse where you rotate the ball yourself. Trackballs take some getting used to. You use trackballs to accomplish the same things you accomplish with a mouse, but they have one advantage over mice: you don't need a desktop to operate a trackball. Some keyboards include trackballs, and one available trackball fits onto the side of those cute little notebook computers, which are discussed in Chapter 13.

The latest wrinkle in the mouse-equivalence game is IBM's Stick Shift, a pointing control device included with its Think Pad notebook computers. This is a little red rod that's positioned right between the G and H keys on the keyboard, where it won't get run over by flying fingers. You put your index finger on the end of this thing and, as you move it, the pointer flies around on-screen. You use your thumb to click buttons on the Stick Shift.

I HATE PCs!

Graphics Tablet

A *graphics tablet* is a neat input device for all you artistic types. Basically, a graphics tablet is a flat, electronically sensitive "page" on which you draw with an electronic "pen." You don't see the result on the tablet, which just stays blank—as if the pen contains no ink. On the contrary, the result appears on-screen. If you're not running a graphics program, the graphics tablet might be able to double as a mouse-like pointing device for all those clicking and dragging maneuvers.

Joy Sticks

A *joystick* is another kind of pointing device and is a must for arcade-action games. It plugs into a *game port*, which your computer might not have. If your computer doesn't have a game port, you need to buy a *game board*, which is an expansion board that fits into one of the empty expansion slots inside the system unit of your computer.

Surge Protectors

(Don't let your system get zapped!)

It's not a pretty subject. But that innocent-looking power receptacle might just be the death of your computer. Everyday current fluctuations (like the ones that cause the lights to flicker when your refrigerator starts) are commonplace, and they can cause your system to crash. What's worse, lightning can cause a massive power surge capable of frying just about anything that's plugged in—even stuff that's turned off.

(If you're experiencing extreme weather, it's always best to unplug the computer or surge protector from the wall socket, just to be completely safe. Why tempt fate?)

To be on the safe side, plug your computer into a surge protector. *Surge protectors* prevent those nasty power surges from affecting your computer.

Checklist

▼ You may see *power strips* that include "surge protection," but don't bet on it if the price is $9.95. Expect to pay more—up to $100—for decent surge protection. It's worth it.

▼ Get a surge protector that has plenty of plugs so that you can plug all your computer equipment into it, including the printer. You can then turn on everything just by flipping the switch on the surge protector.

Uninterruptable Power Supplies

(Data loss is forever)

If you're using your computer for a business or profession, think seriously about getting an uninterruptable power supply (UPS). A UPS includes *surge suppression*, but it offers so much more: to wit, a battery that automatically charges itself. When the power goes out the window, the battery steps in. All the lights go off and the stereo suddenly goes quiet, but you're still in business. You've then got about 10 or 15 minutes to save everything, shut down, go get a brewski, and thank your lucky stars.

Uninterruptable power supplies used to cost a lot of money ($300-$500), but the price has gone down considerably. I'm seeing good units selling for as little as $129.

Tape Backup Drive

(Soothing words for anyone who hates backing up)

You don't get very far in one of these computer books without having a big guilt trip laid on you about Not Backing Up. You know how they go:

> You should back up your work to floppy disks at frequent intervals—preferably, at the end of every operating session.

Boring as such admonitions may be, they're grounded in good sense. Entire businesses have gone belly up because the firm's mailing list, client contacts, or other priceless information got wiped out. And all because the poor dolts didn't back up.

The problem is, it's a pain to back up with floppies.

A *tape backup system* is like the difference between night and day when it comes to backup convenience. Also known as a *tape cartridge drive*, this thing is about the size of a floppy disk drive, and fits in one of your computer's empty drive bays. (A *drive bay* is a place where you can stick a floppy disk drive.) A tape backup system uses removable tape cartridges, which can store up to 250MB of information per tape.

To back up your system with a cartridge tape, you stick in the cartridge, use your backup software, and just forget about it. The tape backup system copies your hard disk's contents to the tape. You take out the tape, and put it away, hoping never to use it. But if your disk crashes, you put in a new disk, and then "play back" your tape. Lo! Your hard disk is

restored, at least up to the moment that you last backed up. But for business, professional, and creative users, that could mean the difference between being in business or out of business.

Tape backup systems used to be expensive ($400-$600), but recently there's been a dramatic price drop. You can get a pretty good tape drive for as little as $220, and cartridges only run you $25 or so.

Sound Boards

(Listen to your error beep in full, digital stereo!)

You've probably noticed that your PC contains a pretty pathetic little speaker, which is only capable of emitting sounds like "beep" (the usual error beep). For more robust sound, you can add a sound board to your system.

A *sound board* is a plug-in expansion board that fits into one of the unoccupied expansion slots inside your computer's system unit.

Checklist

▼ Your programs can't do anything with the sound board unless they've been specially designed to do so. Lots of games include sounds for sound boards. In addition, Microsoft Windows includes sound board support. You can assign specific sounds, which are stored on your hard disk, to specific system events, such as opening a window.

▼ Windows comes with a few sounds built in, but you can buy more. My favorite sound package is Star Trek: The Next Generation Audio Clips, which includes sounds like the briefing room, bridge sounds, the *swish* sound from those cool doors, phasers, and "Red Alert."

▼ Is there a good reason to equip your system with a sound card? Yes. It's called *multimedia*. In brief, multimedia is the use of the computer as a presentation medium that involves video, animation, text, and sound. By adding a sound board and a CD-ROM player to your system, you can take advantage of multimedia. (CD-ROM is discussed in the next section.)

▼ You need speakers, and possibly an amplifier, to hear the sound generated by your sound board. You can plug your PC into your stereo, but chances are it's in another room. If so, you can get self-amplified speakers for as little as $29 each. My favorite techno-junkie catalog, DAK Industries Incorporated (800/325-0800), offers a pair of computer speakers that comes with a subwoofer, so you can add thunderous depths to the tweety highs. The speakers are magnetically shielded, too, so they won't zap your floppy disks.

CAUTION

If you're thinking of getting a sound board, look for one that's compatible with Sound Blaster or Ad Lib, the two most common sound boards. Most programs are designed to work with one or both of these.

CD-ROM Drives and Disks

The typical American household has laid those old vinyl LPs to rest, and taken up with these compact disk player gadgets. You're familiar, probably, with audio compact discs (CDs). What you probably didn't know is that compact discs can also store computer data—and I mean *lots* of computer data, to the tune of over 600MB. Just in case you're curious, that's the equivalent of 17 40MB hard disks.

CD-ROM stands for *compact disc-read-only memory*, which to the ears of technoweenies, perfectly describes what this medium is all about. It's read-only, which means that you can't record anything on these disks (any more than you can record music on audio compact discs). On the positive side, CD-ROM disks hold so much data that an entire encyclopedia can fit on one disk. No joke. This makes CD-ROM an ideal distribution medium for material that takes up a lot of space; sound and pictures, for example, are notorious hogs of disk space.

Checklist

▼ To use CD-ROMs, you need a CD-ROM drive. You can't use your stereo's compact disc player.

▼ There are two kinds of CD-ROM drives, *external* and *internal*. The external kind costs more because it needs its own power supply and case. The internal kind fits into one of those empty drive bays (areas where you can stick a floppy disk drive). If you have a drive bay available, the internal kind is the way to go.

▼ CD-ROM drives vary in *retrieval speed*. The information retrieval speed of a CD-ROM drive is measured in milliseconds (thousandths of a second, abbreviated *ms*). Drives with a retrieval time of 800 ms are very slow; drives with a retrieval time of about 300 ms are much, much better (and lots, lots more expensive).

▼ The CD-ROM drive comes with its own expansion board, which you insert into one of the available expansion slots inside the system unit of your computer.

▼ More and more CD-ROM disks are becoming available. You can get encyclopedias, unabridged dictionaries, world atlases, almanacs of all types, family medical guides, and lots of educational disks.

For what you were about to shell out for your kid's Britannica, you could buy a PC, a CD-ROM drive, and just tons of compact discs. *And* you won't have to sit through those obnoxious Encyclopedia Britannica commercials with the squeaky-voiced kid who should be slapped upside the head.

▼ What's the point of having all this stuff on a compact disc? The computer can search through it—fast. Suppose I want to know what percentage of the human body is made up of water. I type the search terms *body*, *human*, and *water*. Presto! I see the encyclopedia page where this startling fact is revealed.

TIP

If you shop around, you can get some great deals on drives that include a lot of compact discs. Even as I write, a tempting catalog lies before me offering a 340 ms Sony drive with six CDs included. The whole bundle costs less than the list price of the CDs. How can I resist?

Top Ten Least Popular CD-ROM Discs

10. Scenic Metropolitan New Jersey

9. Gunshot Exit Wounds: An Illustrated Emergency Room Guide

8. Ten Easy Steps to an Uncontrolled Nuclear Reaction

7. The Sayings of Chairman Mao (On-Line Edition)

6. The Accordion from A to Z

continues

I HATE PCs!

Top Ten Least Popular CD-ROM Discs, continued

5. Road Kill Recipes from the Rural South

4. Charles Manson's Prison Notebooks (Full Text Edition)

3. A Naturalist's Guide to Common Household Molds and Fungi

2. Family Photo Album of the Brady Bunch

1. Save Big by Making Your Own Casket

Additional, Fascinating Gadgets

The list just goes on and on. And, my Visa bill gets bigger and bigger.

Peripheral	The Scoop
Scanners	These devices look like little, flat photocopying machines. They *scan* a page of graphics or text, converting what they see into a form that your computer can use. You can then include the image in your documents. Some scanners are hand-held, but they're limited to material that's no more than three or four inches wide.
Optical Character Recognition (OCR) Reader	An OCR reader looks just like a scanner, but it has an additional capability: It transforms the text it

Peripheral	The Scoop
	scans into computer-usable text, which you can then edit and modify just as you would modify any text. (A scanner just takes a picture of the text; you can modify the picture only with great difficulty.) The only drawback to OCR readers is that they're not 100-percent accurate. The good ones let you know when they're having difficulty, though. And if you run the text through a spelling checker, you can catch and fix most of the glitches. This is a great timesaving peripheral for anyone who needs to get tons of printed text into the computer.
Digital Camera	You shoot and digitally store up to 32 still pictures, which you then transfer to your PC. Once inside your PC, you can use graphics software to touch up, edit, and print these pictures. You can even combine images to make space-age "montages."
Copy Holder	Probably the only really cheap accessory you can get, this thing clamps onto your monitor and holds up paper so you can see the paper (maybe a handwritten report that you are typing into the computer) while you're working.

continues

I HATE PCs!

Peripheral	The Scoop
Bar Code Reader	You've seen these at the video store—they look like a pencil, but they're designed to read those universal product codes with the bars on them. They transform this printed information into a number that the computer recognizes and matches with additional information (such as price and product description).

EXPERTS ONLY

And the prize for the best computer peripheral goes to...

Get this: you can buy a plug-in expansion board that contains a TV tuner. Plug this into your CATV system, and you can open a window (while you're still working with other Windows applications) to catch up on Oprah.

CHAPTER 12

The Great Communicators

(Modems, Faxes, and Networks)

IN A NUTSHELL

- ▼ What a modem is
- ▼ How people use modems
- ▼ How you can send and receive faxes from your computer
- ▼ What a local area network (LAN) is and what it does

I HATE PCs!

Most people don't realize that computers are used as much for communication as for crunching numbers and printing reports. If you'd like the latest stock quotes and weather, if you need to exchange documents with coworkers in distant regional offices, or if you just like getting involved in a computer equivalent of a late night talk show, your computer can assist you. That is, it can help you when it's suitably equipped. Yes, pull out your Visa card again, because we're talking about more accessories here: modems, fax boards, and networks.

Modems and Their Magic

A *modem* is a computer accessory that allows your computer to send and receive computer signals via the telephone system. If there's a computer on the other end that's also equipped with a modem, the two computers can "talk" to each other and share files. If there's a human on the other end, he's going to hear nothing but annoying honks, beeps, and moans, and you won't even be able to say, "Sorry, wrong number."

Checklist

▼ To get the modem to do anything useful, you need a communications program. But you may not need to buy the program. Lots of modems come with freebie communications programs, and one's included with Microsoft Windows.

▼ You can get two kinds of modems, internal and external. An *internal modem* fits into an empty expansion slot inside your system unit (see Chapter 5). An *external modem* has its own case and power supply, and gets in the way on your desk. It plugs into an unused serial port.

▼ Most modems have two phone jacks, one for the phone line and the other for an extension phone. You can plug your phone into the extension phone jack so that you don't have to give up having a phone in your office.

▼ When you're using your modem, your phone line is tied up. And if someone picks up the phone, your screen shows garbled characters. You could get two phone lines, but this solution is expensive. If you use the modem fairly infrequently, it's usually not too much trouble to just plug it in when you need it.

▼ Modems have varying speeds, rated in bits per second (bps). The standard speed for modems today is 2400 bps; 1200 bps and 300 bps modems are considered obsolete, but they might be OK for occasional use.

▼ A couple terms are specific to ModemSpeak. When you send a file through your modem to someone else's computer, you are *uploading* the file. When you get a file through your modem, you are *downloading* the file.

▼ You can upload and download files of all kinds, including program and data files. When you download a file, you can use it as you would any other file on your computer.

▼ You can also use a modem to get into a dialogue with the computer at the other end of the system. This is sort of like using DOS; you have to type commands, and then you get a reply. With special software on both ends, though, you get menus and other easy-to-use stuff.

"I HATE THIS!"

I can't talk to my modem!

Modems are tough to set up. You have to figure out which serial port they're occupying, which can be something of a trick. And then you have to pull off a trick called *configuring the communication parameters*. By now, you recognize the kind of talk that sends you running for your local computer wizard! Get someone to help you set up your modem and communications software; after that, you can use it without worrying about any of this junk.

Things to Do with Your Modem

(Legal and otherwise)

With your computer linked to the world telephone system, there's no end to what you can do. Most modem activities, though, boil down to the following five.

Sharing Data with a Friend or Coworker

Any two computers equipped with modems can communicate, although this requires a lot of coordination. You have to call, and say, "Hey, Ralph, turn on your modem, and set it to auto-answer; I'm ready to upload that file." People use this a lot to send files back to the office (or home) when they're off traveling with one of those neat little notebook computers (see Chapter 13).

Electronic Mail

Electronic mail (abbreviated *e-mail*) works like this: you use your modem to upload a letter to Fred; it's stored on the electronic mail service's gigantic computer. Later, when Fred contacts the e-mail service, the computer says, "Fred, you have mail." Fred then reads your letter, and can respond, if he likes. The problem is, what if Fred never contacts the service? He won't get the mail. E-mail is only useful when all the parties who are trying to keep in touch agree to *log on* (contact the service) at a set interval, like once a day or once a week.

Calling Information Services

An *information service* is a giant computer that's stuffed with resources for people calling in with their modems. These computers can receive hundreds or even thousands of calls at once. You see a menu with lots of options, such as Weather, Stock Quotes, and Soap Opera Twists. Popular information services include Prodigy, America/Online, CompuServe, and Dow Jones News/Retrieval Service.

To use one of these services, you have to subscribe. You get charged a flat monthly service fee plus additional fees for using stuff such as electronic mail (sending electronic letters to other people using the system), conferences (joining discussion groups on various topics), and having the service send a fax from a file you upload. Fortunately, you don't have to call a long-distance number; the service gives you a local number to call, and handles the long-distance part from there.

Having Fun with Local Bulletin Boards

A *bulletin board* is a do-it-yourself information service that local computer hobbyists set up. All it takes is an unused PC, a modem, and bulletin board software. Most bulletin boards keep huge storehouses of shareware and public domain software, which you can download and use on your computer. (These are discussed in Chapter 17.)

Also available are discussion groups and mail. Many bulletin boards address specific themes or topics, like Hatha Yoga Central or Matchbook Collector's Hotline.

Gaining Unauthorized Access to Corporate and Government Computers

This is a favorite activity of teenage computer zombies, who go by fanciful names such as The Dark Avenger and Satan's Nephew. The object is to thwart the system's defenses. This is, of course, a crime, but this point does not seem to impress itself upon these youthful adventurers, some of whom are subsequently hired by the organizations in question, who need an expert's advice to defend themselves against future attacks.

Top Ten Rejected Bulletin Board Themes

10. Tips for the Socially Clueless

9. Ingrown Toenail Alert

8. Let's Get Even

7. Bambi's Mommy: Support for Guilty Hunters

6. Psychotic Loners On-Line

5. What We've Learned about Our Neighbors by Exploring Their Garbage

4. Recipes from Summer Camp

3. Dates that Ended in Embarrassment

2. It's Nothing a Firearm Wouldn't Solve

1. Processed Cheese Product Hotline

Fax It to the Max!

Fax machines are popping up everywhere, but they aren't cheap—you have to shell out about $500 to get a decent machine. You've probably seen them work: you feed sheets of paper into the machine, which takes a picture of the page line-by-line, transforms the picture into data that can be transmitted over a phone line, and contacts a fax machine at the other end, which then spits out copies of the pages on yucky thermal paper.

Fax machines are expensive. But you can equip your computer with a fax/modem board for about $100. (A *fax/modem board* includes the modem capabilities just discussed, as well as some fax capabilities, too.) By adding a fax/modem board to your computer, you turn the computer into a fax machine for about one-fifth the cost.

Checklist

▼ I hate to puncture this bubble, but there's just one little flaw here. Fax machines include a scanner that can take a picture of an existing document, such as a letter or photograph. Unless you equip your computer with one of the scanner accessories discussed in the previous chapter, you can only send documents that you've created with the computer. You won't be able to send Cousin Ted a copy of that great brochure about the beach house in Bermuda.

continues

I HATE PCs!

CHAPTER 12

Checklist, continued

▼ When you receive a fax, you're receiving a picture. The only thing you can do with this picture is print it or store it. That's true even if the fax is all text. It's still a picture—a picture of some text. You can't get the text into your computer and work with it. For that, you need a modem. Modems can receive files, which you can work with just like any other file on your computer.

▼ Beware of "bargain-basement" deals on fax/modem boards—you could get stuck with a *receive only* fax, which can't send out faxes. You can get a *send and receive* fax/modem board for just a little more money.

▼ Cheap fax/modem boards tend to be a hassle to use. Some people have so much trouble figuring them out that they just give up. The best fax/modem boards, such as the Intel SatisFAXtion 100, cost a bit more than other boards. Check out the software that comes with the fax/modem board before buying.

Networks

(Hello, Central?)

From the beginning, the basic idea of personal computing was to give each individual his or her own computer, and also the freedom to decide how to use it. A great idea. But it did create some problems. Does everybody have to have an expensive printer? How do we share stuff?

These questions stumped the computer geniuses, but they went to work. Their solution? The *local area network* (abbreviated *LAN*, which rhymes with *Dan*). In brief, a local area network is a bunch of cables and connectors that let two or more PCs share peripherals (like printers) and files. All the computers on the network have to be physically connected through special, high-speed cables—the phone line is just too slow. The network allows people to use their PCs quite happily, except when they want to share something.

Why a Network?

One of the most common reasons for creating a network is to share an expensive printer. A network means that all of your coworkers can print gorgeous documents from the same laser printer—thus saving the company thousands of dollars.

Another common reason for creating a network is to share information. In a real estate office, for example, every realtor wants to see the list of currently available properties. It makes sense to keep just one copy of this information and let everyone access it. Also, networks allow you to use electronic mail, which was discussed in the previous section. You write a letter to someone else on the network, and when that person logs on, he is alerted that mail is waiting for him.

Yet another reason for creating networks is to let people use network versions of software. A *network version* of a program like Lotus 1-2-3 is a version that is—you guessed it—designed to work on a network. What this means is that just one copy of the program can be accessed by two or more people at once.

I HATE PCs!

▼ Typically, local area networks link anywhere from a half dozen to several dozen computers.

▼ If you're using a PC in a large, up-to-date corporation bent on effective international competitiveness, you're probably hooked up to a network already. Don't be embarrassed if you didn't know; networks are so slick that they let you use your PC as if the network didn't exist.

▼ If you're connected to a network, you probably have a *network adapter card* in one of your computer's expansion slots. There's also probably a cable coming out of the back of your computer.

▼ Most networks have *file servers*, computers that are completely given over to handling network tasks. Here's where you find the files and programs that everyone shares, and also the programs that help the network to run.

▼ You have to use special commands and procedures to access the network resources, like printers and programs. Because these commands and procedures vary depending on the type of network, you need to get the details from the person in charge of the network. This person is probably called the *network administrator*. If no one is in charge of the network, look out—it's not going to be very reliable!

▼ Possibly, you'll need to log onto the network. This means typing your user name (a moniker that lets electronic mail find you) and password (a secret code that keeps other people from posing as you and doing nefarious things like writing nasty letters to the boss).

▼ In a lot of networks, the network's presence is felt by the appearance of what looks like an extra hard disk—often named drive F—on the system. This drive, which is actually on the file server, is called a *network drive*. The network drive works just like an ordinary hard disk, with all those maddening directories and such. This drive contains the network versions of software you can run. You start these programs just like you would start any program on your hard disk.

Questions to Ask Your Network Administrator

If you have a network, ask the network administrator the following questions:

1. How do I get onto the network? Exactly what do I have to type?

2. What is my user name? Do I have to type a password?

3. Is there a network drive? Which drive is it?

4. How do I access the network printer to print my documents?

5. Are there any programs available on the network? How do I use them?

6. How do I send a file to someone else on the network?

7. Are there any shared files on the network that I should be using?

8. Is there a way I can send a fax through the network?

9. Is this network set up for electronic mail? How do I use it?

10. Don't you think it's dumb that this network is so hard to use?

CHAPTER 13

Laptops, Notebooks, and Palmtops

(Taking It with You)

IN A NUTSHELL

▼ Find out what luggables, laptops, notebooks, and palmtops are—and why they're cool

▼ Get a charge out of examining notebook batteries

▼ Explore the limitations of notebook keyboards

▼ Find out what makes for a quality display in a notebook computer

▼ Examine the pointing devices used with notebooks

▼ Look at ways to connect a notebook to your desktop system

I HATE PCs!

I t's amazing. My 7.7-pound notebook computer, which fits into my slimline briefcase, has all the power of that behemoth system that's taking up two-thirds of my desk back home. And it's portable. I'm writing this right now at 30,000 feet, somewhere over Rapid City, South Dakota. The only problem is, the nosy guy next to me just can't keep his eyes off my screen. I don't mean to be unfriendly, but could you move over one seat so I can use my mouse? Thanks.

If you're thinking about buying a portable computer instead of (or in addition to) a desktop mammoth, or you're just curious about portables, this chapter should prove interesting; it surveys this intriguing, miniature world. And, as you'll discover, some very tiny machines are actually good enough to give your desktop machine serious competition.

From Luggable to Palmtop

My very first computer, way back in 1981, was ostensibly a "portable"—a Kaypro II. In one system unit, you got the computer, the disk drives, and monitor (but the keyboard wasn't built in). The tough, metal case was actually developed for use in the M-1 tank, and it was built on the assumption, apparently, that the enemy would be shooting at it. All this meant weight. Lots of it. The Kaypro weighed in at a hefty 28 pounds. These and similar "portables" earned the derisive epithet "luggable." Mine stayed put, right on my desk. Since that time, the only computers that legitimately earn the epithet "portable" are those that weigh under 12 pounds—and the keyboard must be built in.

BUZZWORDS

PORTABLE COMPUTER

A lightweight, battery-powered PC that includes a keyboard, disk drives, and a display in one compact unit. You can get an AC adapter to run the system from a wall socket, if one's available.

Checklist

▼ The first truly portable computers, averaging about 10 pounds, were called *laptops*. Laptops are still around, but the action has shifted to *notebook computers*. Ten pounds doesn't sound like much, but try carrying around a 10-pound sack of potatoes, and you'll get the idea. You see lots of laptops advertised in Distress Sale catalogs and on the Home Shopping Network. These are cheap, but there's a reason: they're heavy.

▼ Notebook computers weigh in at about 7 pounds, on average, but their key characteristic is their ability to fit inside a briefcase. They're about the size of a college textbook (8 by 11 by 2 inches). Notebooks can give desktop computers serious competition. They offer big, fast hard disks; a single 3.5-inch floppy disk drive; decent screens; and reasonably good keyboards. You can get good accessories, too, such as modems and fax boards. Notebooks are the most popular type of portable computer, but a good notebook costs two to three times what a comparable desktop system costs.

▼ *Subnotebook computers* average about 3 pounds, and are half the thickness of notebook computers. You have to use an external floppy disk drive, and the keyboards are cramped. Some of these

continues

machines could replace a desktop computer, but they tend to use older, outmoded microprocessors, like the 8088 or 80286. This could pose problems if you want to run Windows. These machines can't really replace a desktop computer, unless you only use the computer to write an occasional short letter or memo.

▼ Palmtops weigh in at 1 pound or less. They have little, cramped keyboards, often with keys the size of Chiclet gum. Mostly, they're used for appointment scheduling and expense tracking for busy people "on the go." They're also dearly loved by gadget freaks. Some can run DOS and DOS applications, though, so they make sense if you need to use something like Lotus 1-2-3 in the field.

▼ The future will see something called the Personal Digital Assistant (PDA), a palmtop without a keyboard. You'll work it by "writing" on the screen; the computer will decode your writing and do things like help you keep appointments, send faxes via cellular phone connections, and perform all sorts of space-age stuff. But the future isn't far off, as you can see the next time a UPS driver delivers a package—UPS is already using a PDA to record deliveries.

▼ Computers keep getting smaller; unfortunately, fingers don't. A notebook computer—with normal-sized keys—is the best bet if you plan to do a lot of typing.

▼ Because notebooks are by far the most popular portables these days, I'll just use the term *notebook* generically to refer to portable computers in general.

TIP

Thinking of using your notebook outside? It sounds great, doesn't it? But remember, dust, dirt, sand, and temperature extremes are murder on computers. If it's mild enough for you to be comfortable, it's mild enough for your computer. Otherwise, leave the computer at home. Also, don't leave your notebook computer in the car on a sunny day.

Top Ten Rejected Notebook Computer Names

10. Peewee Pixel Hound

9. DataDwarf Deluxe

8. The Dashing Diminutive

7. Peerless Processing Pygmy

6. Byte Bantam

5. SuperShrunk II

4. IBM InfiniTesimal (IT)

3. Le Petite Portable Peckboard

2. TinyTyper

1. Wee Workstation

"My Battery's Dead!"

It sounds great, doesn't it? Instead of being stuck at your desk, you could be sitting in that big rocking chair, watching the boats go by on the Rappahannock and working with that trendy new notebook computer. Unless you have a really long extension cord, though, you're dependent on the computer's batteries. And they run down pretty fast. With today's feature-packed systems, expect a battery life of only four to five hours for monochrome systems. With color screens, the figure drops to only two to three hours, maximum.

Battery basics

▼ Most notebooks use nickel-cadmium (NiCad) batteries. They're rechargeable, but they have some drawbacks. For one thing, cadmium is incredibly toxic, and poses a hazard to children and to the environment. The latest battery technology is the nickel hydride (NiMH) battery, which is more expensive, but is non-toxic.

▼ To recharge your battery, use the recharger supplied with the system.

▼ Some applications are *notebook smart*—they display a message warning you if the battery's low. Be sure to save your work when you see this message. Then you can slip in a fresh battery (if you have one), or charge the dead one.

▼ Portables that conform to the Advanced Power Management (APM) specification use about 25 percent less power. If you're shopping for a notebook, look for a machine that has this feature.

▼ The latest wrinkle in microprocessors is the low-power CPU, such as the Intel 386SL and 486SL, which consumes a lot less power. If you're shopping for a system, look for one that has one of these microprocessors.

I HATE PCs!

CAUTION

Beware the massive AC adapter. What could be more ridiculous than a 6-pound notebook that comes with a 4-pound AC adapter? This is something most people don't think of until they've purchased their systems—and then they're stuck carrying the AC adapter around with them, nullifying any advantage they may have gained by getting a notebook that's a pound or two lighter than the competition.

"This Keyboard Stinks!"

Notebook keyboards are improving, but this is still an area that gives a lot of portable computer users fits. Even with the best keyboards, the key layout will differ from the keyboard you're using at the office (or at home). And some notebooks have just *terrible* keyboards. If you're thinking of buying, try out the keyboard first!

Awful things about notebook keyboards

▼ I'm sure you've never pondered *key travel*, the distance the key travels when you press it down. Believe me, I hadn't. But a lot of notebook computers don't have enough travel distance, leaving you wondering whether you've really depressed the key. The best notebook keyboards have something called *full travel*, which isn't about portability—it means the keys have the same travel distance as a real keyboard.

▼ Some notebook keyboards lack function keys. You can still use commands that employ function keys, but you'll have to press some bizarre, inconvenient key combination to do so. The best notebook keyboards have a full row of function keys (F1 through F12).

continues

Awful things about notebook keyboards, continued

▼ Avoid any notebook keyboard that lays out the cursor-movement keys in anything other than the inverted T pattern your desktop keyboard uses. A nice feature: Home, End, Page Up, and Page Down keys.

▼ The location of the Ctrl and Alt keys varies wildly on notebook keyboards. If you're shopping for a notebook computer, look for one that lays out the Ctrl and Alt keys the same way your desktop computer keyboard does. Because you use these keys constantly, you don't want to relearn their locations.

"I HATE THIS!"

"No, it isn't a bomb! It's a computer!" "Oh, yeah? Prove it!"

If you plan to travel with your laptop, get ready for several gigantic hassles. The first begins at the security gate of the airport. Your innocent little notebook computer is under suspicion of being a murderous device filled with plastic explosives, so you'll be asked to turn it on (proving, thereby, that it's really a computer, and not a bomb). When you're on the plane, you may find that some airlines aren't happy about the use of electronic devices, which might interfere with the plane's radio. (That wouldn't be good for you or the computer, would it?) Generally, the smaller the plane, the more likely they'll be antsy about this. Bear in mind that you may be asked to shut down your system.

"The Display's Worse Than the Keyboard!"

Notebook computers don't use the same heavy (but high-quality) display technology found in desktop systems. They use lightweight, low-power screens instead. There are exceptions, but most notebooks use *liquid-crystal display* (LCD) screens. LCD displays use the same, basic principles as the displays in electronic watches and calculators. LCD screens are getting better, but in general they're much slower than their desktop counterparts—so slow, in fact, that in some systems, the mouse pointer gets lost when you move it too quickly. And they're also hard to see, unless the screen is lit in ways that gobble up power very quickly. The same advice goes for displays as for keyboards—don't buy a notebook computer without seeing the display in action.

What to look for in a notebook display

▼ LCD displays don't produce any light by themselves. If the screen isn't lit, you can't even see the display unless you're working in a well-lit area. And, you have to get the angle just right on the re-flected light. On the positive side, unlit LCD displays consume very little power, and systems with these displays often offer as much as six hours of computing on one battery charge.

▼ Backlit LCD displays are much easier to read when the light isn't good, but they consume a lot more power.

▼ Very few systems (except palmtops and subnotebooks) still offer old, obsolete CGA displays. Today's systems have VGA displays, making them compatible with almost all software. (For more infor-mation on this CGA and VGA palaver, see Chapter 8.)

continues

What to look for in a notebook display, continued

▼ LCD screens don't *refresh* (repaint) the screen image at anything near the speed of desktop displays, causing irritating problems with blurring. If you move the mouse pointer too fast, you may not be able to see it until it stops.

▼ Backlit *supertwist* LCD screens offer improved performance, but at a higher price. The latest (and most expensive) display technology is the *active matrix* screen, which approaches the quality of desktop displays. Active matrix screens are available in both gray scale and color versions.

▼ Monochrome (black and white) systems are passé; today's systems offer gray scale displays that try to reproduce colors with 32 or 64 shades of gray. Unfortunately, most of them don't do a very good job, which creates a good argument for a color display.

▼ The cheapest color displays are called *passive matrix* displays. These are OK but some people don't like the "Impressionist" quality of the colors, which are pastels rather than strong, bright primaries.

▼ The best notebook displays are *active-matrix color* displays. A display recently developed jointly by IBM and Toshiba measures 10.4 inches diagonally, and produces a rich, beautiful display. Of course, this beauty does come with a pretty hefty price tag.

"Please, Give Me My Mouse Back!"

Yet another area of deficiency in most laptops: pointing devices. Most come with a mouse port, which lets you plug in the same type of mouse you use with your desktop computer. But where are you going to roll it?

If you're on a plane, you'll have to use the leg of the guy sitting next to you, which might not be appreciated.

To solve this problem, notebooks offer a variety of solutions, but none of them are particularly satisfactory. Some systems come with tiny, built-in trackballs that don't offer enough control to be usable. Another solution: Microsoft's BallPoint, a trackball that clamps onto the side of your notebook's keyboard. This fix is better than a built-in trackball, but not by much. The latest gizmo is IBM's TrackPoint II, a little red stick shift offered with the company's Think Pad computers. The TrackPoint juts out between the G and H keys. You move the pointer by controlling this stick with your index finger, but it takes some getting used to.

Making Connections

Notebook computers are great for making connections—use one at any airport, and every nerd within hailing distance will come over and say, "Gee, that's a great display. What's your hard disk's access time?" until you finally give up working and pull out *People Magazine*. Actually, what I had in mind for this section was *external connections*—connecting to items like external monitors.

Getting connected

▼ Look for a system with an external VGA and keyboard connector. At home, you can use these to transform your notebook into a "real" computer.

▼ You can get a built-in modem or fax/modem for most notebooks. (Chapter 12 tells you a bit more about modems and fax/modems.)

continues

▼ I don't recommend computing and driving at the same time, but you can get an adapter cord that lets you hook up your notebook to your car's cigarette lighter. This would be great for private eyes on stakeouts.

▼ Most notebook computers have a standard printer port. (Flip to Chapter 5 for information about ports.) You can even get portable printers, but they're a hassle to use and they double the weight of the junk you're carrying around. Your best bet is to print at home, or to bring a cable to hook up with friendly printers that you chance to meet on the road.

▼ The ultimate in connectability is the *docking system*. No, this isn't something from *Deep Space 9*. A docking system looks like a desktop computer—it has a monitor, disk drives, a decent keyboard, and connections for printers and the like—except that you can slide your notebook computer right into it. Instantly and automatically, your notebook is hooked up to the monitor, printer, disk drives, and keyboard.

▼ If you don't have a docking system, you can get utility software that lets you connect your notebook to your desktop system via a connector cord. Once the connection is established, the software lets you access the desktop computer's hard disk as if it were part of the notebook computer itself.

PART III

Software

Includes:

CHAPTER 14

Directory Assistance

IN A NUTSHELL

▼ What files are and how to name them

▼ How to make sense of directory concepts

▼ What the current directory is and why it matters a lot

▼ How to decode path names (and when to use them)

▼ What wild cards are and how they're used

▼ How to work with files in other directories or drives

Welcome to the software section of *I Hate PCs*, where you probably expected me to segue right into using games like King's Quest or Flight Simulator. But there are some preliminaries to take care of. Before you can get to the fun stuff—application software—you first need to learn about the less-than-fun stuff, like organizing, naming, and maintaining files.

This chapter discusses files, file names, and directories—necessary subjects for any DOS or Windows user. "What?" Ask the Windows users, "We have to know this horrible DOS stuff too?" Yup. Windows makes DOS pretty, but underneath Windows is DOS, and its restrictions and peculiarities can be seen beneath all the colorful on-screen Windows action. The better you understand files, and how they're named, and where they're stored, the less chance you'll get so frustrated that you "caress your system with a baseball bat," as we politely term it.

The next chapter goes into more basics of managing files using DOS, while Chapter 16 covers the same topics for Windows users. But this chapter covers grunt-level system management basics that both DOS and Windows users should know.

Files

(And those dratted file names)

Everything on your computer—hard disk or floppy disk—is stored in a *file*. And every file has a name. Some of the files are already on the disk—for instance, program files. Some files are created when you use a program. When you type and save a memo, it is stored as a file.

BUZZWORDS

FILE

A unit of related stuff that is stored on disk. There are two types of files. *Program files* contain instructions the computer can follow; *data files* contain your work. Every file has its own, unique name.

Checklist

▼ File names consist of two parts: a "first" name and a "last" name. You use a period to separate the two names.

▼ The file must have a first name, but it doesn't need a last name. Hey! We're on a first-name basis here, inside the computer!

▼ The first name can have up to 8 characters, but it doesn't have to use this many. The last name can have up to 3 characters, but it doesn't have to use all three.

▼ You can use the last name, called an *extension*, to show how files are related (just like your last name connects you to your family members). You might have .DOC files for document files and .WKS files for worksheet files.

▼ Programs always have an .EXE, .COM, or .BAT extension.

▼ Stick to using letters and numbers in your file names. Except for that period between the first and last name, avoid punctuation.

▼ You can't use spaces in a DOS file name, but some users like to fake it by typing an underscore instead of a space (SHUT_UP.DOS).

continues

▼ Users who are in the know let their applications assign extensions automatically. Some applications are bossy and prefer that you let them assign the extension. Don't fight it; it's a losing battle, and you'll need to conserve your energy for more important DOS operations—like shaking your fist at the screen.

▼ A commonly used extension for text files is .TXT. A text file contains nothing but the standard DOS keyboard characters, without any of the gibberish that programs add to your files.

EXPERTS ONLY

Diligent readers can discover herein exactly which characters may and may not be used in DOS file names

You can't use spaces, commas, backslashes, or periods within the file name. (You must use a period, though, to separate the file name from the extension.) You can use any of these characters:

$$ \_ \, \char94 \, \$ \sim ! \# \% \& - \{ \} @ `` ( ) $$

Why Directories, Anyway?

In brief, a *directory* is a section of your hard disk that has been set aside for storing files of a certain type, like all the letters you've written to your boss over the years asking for a raise. Chances are that you're working with a hard disk big enough to hold tens of thousands of files—and somehow, they've got to be organized.

BUZZWORDS

DIRECTORY

A section of your hard disk that has been set apart for storing files of a certain type (such as recipes or WordPerfect program files).

Suppose that you have one giant folder that holds all 6,000 of the letters you've typed in the last three years. Even if the letters are alphabetized, it would still be difficult to find the letter you need when you need it. Instead, you would be better off keeping the letters in various folders organized logically, perhaps by date or recipient or subject.

Storing data on a computer is the same way—it's much better to put your files in separate directories. For example, you can put all your recipes in a directory called \RECIPES, your poems in a directory called \POEMS, and your enemies list in a directory called \REVENGE. You can create your own directories (and delete them, too), as detailed in the next two chapters.

EXPERTS ONLY

Read this if you're curious to know why all those directories that you didn't create are on your disk

Directories aren't just for your files. Programs like to have their own directories, too; a typical program comes with dozens—or even hundreds—of support files. A lot of programs won't run unless all those support files are right there, in the same directory. That's why the SETUP or INSTALL utilities you use to install a program usually create a new directory to store the program in. (Flip to Chapter 18 if you want to know more about installing new programs.) For example, the DOS SETUP program creates a directory called—you guessed it—\DOS. (That funny backslash tells DOS that the next word is the name of the directory—more about this later.)

The Famous Directory Tree

In the fanciful imagination of DOS's creators, the directory structure of DOS is said to resemble a tree—an upside-down tree, with the root at the top and the branches at the bottom. The following illustration conveys this bizarre idea:

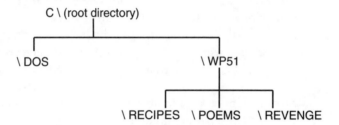

Checklist

▼ The root directory provides the "trunk" from which all the other directories branch out. The root directory, poor thing, doesn't get to have a name; it's indicated only by a solitary backslash (\ ).

▼ Every directory can have directories within it. In this tree, the root directory has two directories: \DOS and \WP51 (the WordPerfect directory). \WP51, in turn, contains three directories: \RECIPES, \POEMS, and \REVENGE.

▼ Note that every directory name must have a backslash in front of it—and that's true even if you string together two or more directory names.

▼ What are *subdirectories*? Basically the same as directories. Some-times this term is used to talk about the relation between two directories. When a directory is placed within another directory, like \RECIPES within \WP51, the one that's within is called a *subdirectory*. Technically, all directories are subdirectories of the root directory. The bottom line is that the terms subdirectory and directory mean the same thing.

BUZZWORDS

PARENT/CHILD DIRECTORY

There's another way to describe the directory-subdirectory relationship. You might run into references to the *parent di-rectory* and its *children*, the subdirectories. The *child direc-tory* is the subdirectory within the *parent directory*.

One Directory at a Time

Why, you're probably wondering, must I learn about directories? The short answer: You need to understand directories so that you can tell your programs where to find files. To elaborate that concept a little, consider that only *one* directory is current at a time. (This directory, oddly enough, is called the *current directory*.)

What does *current* mean? It doesn't mean *up-to-date*. It doesn't have anything to do with electricity. What it means is that DOS or Windows will assume that your file-related command affects the current directory, unless you tell it otherwise.

This simple fact has a number of discouraging implications, all of which add up to not being able to find files on your disk. Let's examine a very common one.

Suppose that you're using a program, and you choose a command that says to the computer, in effect, "Nuke the file called JUNK.DOC." Well, the computer goes hunting in the current directory for JUNK.DOC— but what if it's not there? You get a message like, `File not found`. But that's not true; the file *does* exist! It's just located in another directory.

This concept is like trying to find a love letter that you have stored in the Love Letters manila folder, but you keep looking for it in the Insurance folder. Even though the letter does exist, you will never in a million years find it in the Insurance folder. Likewise, for your program to be able to find a file, you must type the correct path name, and you may even have to type a drive specification. The following section goes into these tedious subjects. Cheer up, this will all be over soon.

Path Names

("Is this the road to Rome?")

Let's say you've created a file called IQUIT.DOC, and it's located in the directory C:\MEMOS\BOSS. The current directory, though, is C:\WP51. When you try to retrieve the file, you get a message like `File not found`.

In such situations, you need to supply the *path name*. The path name tells the computer how to navigate your disk's directory structure in

order to arrive at the desired location. Here's the path name you'd need to supply in order to retrieve IQUIT.DOC:

C:\MEMOS\BOSS\IQUIT.DOC

That ought to do the trick.

▼ The C: part indicates the drive. A drive specification is a letter (like A, B, C, and so on) that refers to a disk drive in your system, followed by a colon (:). The colon is necessary. There's never a space after the colon. A complete *drive specification* looks like A: or B:.

▼ The first backslash indicates the root directory.

▼ MEMOS is the first directory, BOSS is a subdirectory within that directory. You use backslashes to separate the directory names. You also use a backslash between the last directory name and the file name.

▼ No spaces, please, anywhere in a path name.

▼ Don't confuse the backslash (\) with the foreslash (/). Or with a *backlash*, which is what PC designers ought to get for forcing millions of innocent people to have to read boring technical stuff like this.

▼ When you combine a drive specification, a path name, and a file name, you get a *filespec*—short for *file specification*, a complete statement of a file's location.

Those Wacky Wild Cards

(Deal me in)

There's just one more piece of knowledge you need to deal with your hard disk effectively: wild cards.

In poker, the deuce usually is a wild card; it can stand for any other card. If you have three queens, for example, you would want the deuce to stand for a queen.

You can use wild cards the same way in DOS and Windows: to match characters in a file name. Doing so enables you to group files together. You can type commands that say, in effect, "Show me all the files that have the extension DOC." Wild cards are frequently used when retrieving files, copying files, moving files, and—with caution—deleting files.

CAUTION

> You can do a lot of damage with the DOS command DEL *.*, which says, "Delete everything in the current directory." Be careful when using wild cards with DEL. If you try using this command, DOS steps in to ask, "All files in the directory will be deleted! Are you sure (Y/N)?" If you're not sure, press N for No and press Enter.

In DOS and Windows, you can use two wild cards: ? and *. The ? matches any single character. The * matches any number of characters. Here are some examples:

▼ The wild card expression LETTER?.DOC groups all of the following: LETTER1.DOC, LETTER2.DOC, LETTER3.DOC, and so on, up to LETTER9.DOC. But it won't include LETTER10.DOC in the group because the ? wild card only stands for *one* character.

▼ The wild card expression LET*.DOC groups all the files just mentioned. That's because the * wild card stands for any number of characters.

▼ The wild card expression LETTER.* groups LETTER.DOC, LETTER.TXT, and LETTER.BAK.

▼ The wild card expression ???.??? finds any files with a three-letter file name and a three-letter extension (such as SIN.DOC, FUN.TXT, or TOI.JON).

▼ The wild card expression *.* (pronounced "star-dot-star") stands for all files.

Changing Directories

To change to a directory, just type **CD** followed by the directory name. For instance, to change to C:\WP51 from C:\, type **CD WP51** and press Enter.

To change to a subdirectory of the current directory, just type the directory name without the backslash. For example, to change to C:\WP51\POEMS\CATTLE from the C:\WP51\POEMS directory, just type **CD CATTLE** and press Enter.

To get right back up to the parent directory, type **CD..** and press Enter. Those two little dots, incidentally, stand for *parent directory*. That's why there are two. One stands for Momma, and the other stands for Papa.

To change to the root directory, type **CD** and press Enter.

▼ You can't use CD to change to a directory on another drive. You must change drives first, as explained in Chapter 15.

▼ If you see the `Invalid directory` message, check your typing. You probably forgot the space after CD or mistyped the directory or path name.

Top Ten Problems if Starship Enterprise Computer Ran DOS

10. Away team beamed to wrong planet due to typing error

9. Can't find file containing recipe for Romulan ale

8. `Load torpedo and press any key when ready` message takes thrill out of space battles

7. Captain's personal log accidentally rerouted to public address system

6. McCoy often heard exclaiming, "Dammit, Jim—I'm a doctor, not a computer nerd!"

5. Odd-sized floppy disks only available from Ferengi

4. Non-graphics display unable to show cool Star Fleet insignia

3. `Insufficient memory` message appears when trying to run ShieldsUp application and PHASER.EXE at same time

2. `File not found` message is only explanation when away team fails to materialize on transporter pad

1. Accidentally reformatted disk containing navigation data

This Is All a Bit Easier with Windows, But...

This section is for Windows users who are wondering how all this DOS stuff about directories, file names, drive specifications, and wild cards applies to them. I mean, isn't Windows supposed to be *easy*?

Well, Windows can get you out of part of the DOS hassle: specifically, typing those pesky path names. Here's why. When you're retrieving an existing file with Windows, you see a dialog box that, no matter which application you're using, has pretty much the same features for opening (retrieving) existing files. (A *dialog box* is an on-screen box that appears when the program needs more information from you.) This dialog box lets you click on things to select the current drive, directory, and file that you want. But you will still need to understand directories, file names, and wild cards to use Windows.

The following shows the Open dialog box that appears when you retrieve an existing file with Microsoft Word for Windows, a popular Windows word processing program.

Opening files with Microsoft Word for Windows.

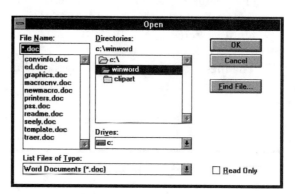

▼ The specifics of how to use this dialog box aren't important here; what's important are the basic concepts of drives, directories, file names, and wild cards, and how they're used in Windows.

▼ Under Drives, you see the current drive. You can change the current drive by clicking on the down arrow. Then click on the drive letter that you want. You then see the directories and files on the new drive.

▼ Under Directories, you see the current directory for the drive that's selected in the Drives box. You can use the directories list under the current directory to change the current directory; just click away at those pictures of folders.

▼ Under File Name, you see a file mask that uses a wild card: *.DOC. This means that only files that have the DOC extension will be displayed. Why? Word automatically assigns this extension to the files you create with Word. And since you're using Word, the program naturally assumes that you want to retrieve Word files. (You can retrieve other kinds of files with Word, but they might look funny on-screen.)

▼ The files list under the File Name box shows the DOC files in the current directory.

▼ Chapter 16 delves into the magic and mystery of Windows file management. You can just skip the next chapter if you like.

CHAPTER 15

DOS
(Those Ol' Operating System Blues)

IN A NUTSHELL

▼ What an operating system is and why
  it's needed

▼ The lowdown on typing DOS
  commands

▼ How to change drives

▼ How to tell which version
  of DOS you're using

▼ How to clear the screen

▼ How to look at the contents
  of a file

▼ How to create directories

▼ How to delete files

▼ How to "undelete" files you
  shouldn't have deleted

▼ How to copy, move, and rename
  files

▼ How to find a missing file

This chapter is for anyone who's using DOS. (Turn to the next chapter if Windows starts automatically when you switch on your computer.) In this chapter, you learn basic file maintenance—looking at files, copying files, moving files, deleting files. Anytime you have a question about how DOS handles any of this file maintenance stuff, just refer to this chapter.

TIP

If the terms *files* and *directories* are leaving your head spinning, take a look at Chapter 14.

What on Earth Is an "Operating System"?

Every computer needs an *operating system*, a program that makes all the computer's components work together in a harmonious, gentlemanly way (they say, "After you, my fine fellow," and "Please, feel free to partake of this file"). The operating system (OS) also provides an interface with the user.

BUZZWORDS

INTERFACE

An *interface* is the part of the program that deals with the user's incessant demands, such as "Delete this file—and I said Now!" and talks back by saying things like, "Not now. I have a headache."

The operating system for PCs is MS-DOS, called *DOS* for short. The MS part stands for Microsoft, which has made big bucks selling copies of DOS with every one of those zillions of PCs now in existence. *DOS* stands for *Disk Operating System*, which pretty much describes how DOS

222

comes across to the user. You use DOS, mainly, to do stuff with your computer's disk drives. And the stuff you do is called *system maintenance*.

System maintenance is a necessary evil of using the computer. It mainly involves working with files—primarily your files, the ones that contain your work. (These are called *data files*.) You can look at them, copy them, and delete them. You can move them, and yes, you can lose them. With any luck, you can find them again.

How Do You Use DOS?

Pretty simple: You type commands at the DOS prompt (that C> or C:\> thing), and you get a result—or an error message. The *error message* indicates that the system wasn't able to carry out your command. In any decent dictatorship, this type of behavior would simply be judged as insubordination and a note would be made in the appropriate record. Unfortunately, this system doesn't work when you're using DOS because DOS is holding all the cards. You either figure out what's wrong, or you can't get to your files. Fortunately, the problem's usually pretty easy to solve.

DOS has zero tolerance for creativity and flourish when you're typing commands. You must type DOS commands exactly right—the command name (like DIR or CLS) *must* be spelled correctly. You *must* put spaces where they're required, and you *must* leave them out where they're not required. You *must* put all the parts of the command in the right order. Got all that?

About the only thing you can ad-lib is capitalization. You can type **diR**, **DIr**, or any other variation, and the command will still work—DOS ignores case. (Here, I'm putting all the DOS commands in capital letters so they'll stick out better. But you can type them in lowercase if you want.)

CHAPTER 15

Changing Drives

Only one drive can be current (*active*) at a time. When a disk drive is *current*, DOS assumes that this is the drive you want to do things to. For example, if you type **DIR** while drive C is current, DOS lists for you all the files and directories on drive C. If you want to look at something on another drive—in most cases, a floppy drive—you need to make *that* drive current.

To make a floppy drive current, insert a disk into the drive. Then just type the drive letter, type a colon, and press Enter. To make drive A current, for example, type **A:** and press Enter. The prompt then shows the current drive:

    A:\>

To get back to drive C, you type **C:** and press Enter.

"I HATE THIS!"

I'm not ready!

When you activate drive A, you may see the following message:

    Not ready reading drive A
    Abort, Retry, Fail?

What's wrong? There's no disk in the drive, or the drive door isn't latched. DOS cannot look at floppy drives unless there is a disk in them. Insert a disk into the drive, close the latch (if the drive has a latch), and press R to retry the command.

"I HATE THIS!"

You also might see this message:

```
General failure reading drive A
Abort, Retry, Fail?
```

This means that the disk is not formatted or ready for use.
The mystery of formatting is revealed in Chapter 7.

And Which Version Are *You* Using?

It's inevitable that someone some time will ask you "What version of
DOS do you have?" Tech support people are big on knowing your ver-
sion of DOS. Also, when you buy new programs, you need to know the
version of DOS because some programs only run with certain versions of
DOS. To find out what version you're using, type **VER** and press Enter.
You see something like this on-screen:

```
MS-DOS Version 6.00
```

(Version 6 is the most recent version of DOS.)

Clearing the Screen of Inflammatory or Embarrassing Messages

Sometimes you will try the same command over and over, and the results of your efforts (such as `Bad command or file name`) will be clearly
displayed on-screen for everyone to see. To cover up any embarrassing
on-screen backtalk, type **CLS** and press Enter.

Peeking at a File's Contents

When hunting for a file, you may not be able to tell by the cryptic name whether you've got the file you want. The TYPE command lets you take a little peek at the file's contents.

To peek at a file's contents, type **TYPE** followed by a space and the name of the file. For example, to peek at the POEM1.DOC document, type **TYPE POEM1.DOC** and press Enter.

Checklist

▼ If you created the file by using an application program such as WordPerfect or Lotus 1-2-3, don't count on seeing your document the way it last looked on-screen. DOS can display only *text*. It can't display formatting changes such as bold, italic, and so on. You may see lots of ridiculous-looking symbols, such as happy faces, staves, knives, Greek symbols, and card suits (clubs, hearts, and so on). You're looking into the internal world of computer information, a world of happy warriors and gamblers who speak Greek. The file might contain enough recognizable text that you can tell whether you've indeed found the document that you want.

▼ If the file doesn't exist in the current directory, you see the `File not found` message. Remember that the file might exist in *another* directory. You can change directories and try again, or type the path name, as explained in the next section.

▼ If you hear a beep when DOS displays the file, the file contains funny computer stuff in addition to text. Don't worry; you haven't hurt the file or your computer. To stop the display, hold down the Ctrl key and press Break. (Break is also labeled *Pause*.)

Technical Babble about Path Names

When you type a command, DOS assumes that you want the command carried out in the current drive or directory. If the current directory is C:\DOCS, for example, DOS will use this directory when you tell it to do something. (See Chapter 14 for an explanation of this "directory" stuff.)

But what if you want something done on another drive or directory? You can change drives or directories so that the one you want to affect is current. Simple enough. Or you can add *path* information. This information tells DOS which "path" to follow on the great mythical hunt for a file.

Here's an example. Suppose the current directory is \NOVELS, and you want to peek at a file called POEM1.DOC that's in the directory called \POEMS. You type the following:

TYPE \POEMS\POEM1.DOC

Note that there's a space after TYPE, but no other spaces. There's a backslash before and after the directory name (POEMS).

You can also add drive names to the file name, as in this example:

TYPE A:\OLDJUNK\VAPID.DOC

This command tells DOS, "Let me peek at the file called VAPID.DOC that's in the directory called OLDJUNK, which you'll find on the disk in drive A."

Checklist

▼ When you type a file name that includes the drive and directory information as well as the name of the file, you've typed a *filespec*. You'll use filespecs a lot when you use DOS's file-management commands, such as COPY, DEL, and RENAME.

▼ Remember, no spaces within a filespec.

▼ You can create directories within directories. Suppose, for example, that you create a directory called \TEDIOUS within the directory \TASKS. A filespec for a file called JUNK.DOC in the \TEDIOUS directory would look like this: C:\TASKS\TEDIOUS\JUNK.DOC.

▼ See Chapter 14 for more information about directories and path names.

BUZZWORDS

FILESPEC

A file name that includes all the information DOS needs to figure out where the file's located, including its drive and directory location.

Making Directories

With all this talk of directories, you're probably wondering how they are created. To create a directory, change to the directory where you want the new directory to be housed. For example, to create a directory called PIGEONS within the POEMS directory, you change to the POEMS directory.

Then type the MD command. To create the PIGEONS directory, type MD PIGEONS and press Enter. Note that there's a space between MD and the directory name.

TIP

> To remember the command to use (MD), think of **M**ake **D**irectory.

Checklist

▼ You can also type **MKDIR** if typing unnecessary characters at the DOS prompt really turns you on.

▼ If you see the message `Bad command or file name`, check your typing. You probably forgot the space after MD.

▼ Directory names obey the same structure as DOS file names: 8-character first name, period, 3-character last name (extension). I wouldn't recommend adding extensions to directory names, however; it makes path names even more laborious to type. Also, when you use DIR, you'll have a tougher time telling the difference between files and directories.

Deleting a File

Disks fill up all too quickly. When you're sure you no longer need an old file that contains one of your documents, delete it. (Then, according to Murphy's Law, you will immediately and desperately need the file.)

CHAPTER 15

CAUTION

Don't delete any files associated with a program, even ones that *look like* they're not all that special. Appearances can be deceiving. Many programs won't run unless dozens or even hundreds of innocent-looking, but vital, files are present.

TIP

If you are unsure whether you'll need a file, copy it to a floppy disk. Then delete the file from the hard disk. (The corollary to the previous Murphy's Law states that making a backup of files assures that the files will never again be needed.)

To delete a file, you use the DEL command. Type the command, a space, and then the file name. Then press Enter. To delete the STICKIT.DOC file, you type **DEL STICKIT.DOC** and press Enter.

Checklist

▼ If the file isn't in the current drive or directory, you have to add the drive and path information so that you've typed a complete filespec—for instance,

    DEL A:\MEMOS\STICKIT.DOC

▼ When you use DEL, it does its thing without giving you any confirmation, which is a little disturbing. You'd think you'd see a message such as `Uh-oh. You just deleted a file. I hope you were sure that you didn't need it.` But there's nothing. Zip. The file's gone, and that's that.

▼ If you would like a second chance to think through the deletion, use the /p switch, like this:

DEL STICKIT.DOC /p

The /p switch with the DEL command turns on an option that tells DOS to ask you to confirm that you want to delete a file. When you see the message, `Delete (Y/N)?`, press Y to confirm the deletion, or N to forget the whole thing and leave the file undisturbed.

BUZZWORDS

SWITCH

In DOS, a *switch* is an option that you add to a command by typing a slash mark (/) followed by a letter, like **/p**.

Deleting a Group of Files

You can use the DOS wild cards to delete more than one file at a time. (If you're wild about learning more, flip back to Chapter 14.) Use caution when you use wild cards with DEL, however. This command can really wipe out a lot of files, and if you haven't thought through what you're doing, you could lose a lot of your data! Here are some examples:

Command	What the Command Does
DEL *.YOU	This command deletes every file that has the extension YOU, such as LOVE.YOU, HATE.YOU, and DANG.YOU. As you can

continues

I HATE PCs!

Command	What the Command Does
	imagine, a command like this one can cause a lot of grief. What if one of those DOC files contains the Great American Novel?
DEL POEM.*	This command deletes any file named POEM, no matter what the extension. (POEM.DOC, POEM.TX, and POEM.BAD will all fall prey.)
DEL *.*	This command deletes all files in the current directory.

CAUTION

If you type **DEL *.***, you're doing something pretty drastic: deleting all the files in the current directory. After you press Enter, you see a message asking you to confirm the deletion. Press Y to proceed or N to cancel the command, and press Enter. Be careful!

Recovering from an Accidental Deletion

Sooner or later, you will accidentally delete a very, very precious file—one that would take hours, days, or even weeks of work to re-create. You will regret ever having used the computer. Chin up. You may be able to recover the deleted files. The key lies in the UNDELETE command.

There's one catch to the happy news about UNDELETE: You must be using Version 5 of DOS or later.

I HATE PCs!

CHAPTER 15

To undelete a file, type **UNDELETE**, a space, and then the file name you want to undelete. For example, to undelete PRECIOUS.DOC, type **UNDELETE PRECIOUS.DOC** and press Enter.

You'll see a file name like this:

```
?RECIOUS.DOC
```

DOS then prompts you, `Undelete (Y/N)?` Press Y. Then type the first character of the file name, which DOS has managed to lose. (Everything else in the file should be OK.)

If DOS can delete the file, you see the message `File successfully deleted`. If DOS can't undelete the file, you see a message such as `The data contained in the first cluster of this directory has been overwritten or corrupted`.

Checklist

▼ Undelete the file right away. If you delay, DOS may overwrite the file with new data, and then it's gone for good.

▼ If you can't remember the name of the file, type **UNDELETE** and press Enter. DOS will go through each file that has been deleted. Press N until the file you want to undelete is listed. Then press Y. You are prompted for the first character of the file name. Type it, and the file is undeleted.

Making a Copy of a File

Copying comes in handy when you want to give a file to someone else or when you want to keep an extra copy for yourself. It's easy to copy a file.

Suppose that you want to make a copy of the first chapter of your path-breaking first novel, NOVEL01.DOC. You type the following:

COPY NOVEL01.DOC NOVEL01.BAK

This command creates a copy of the file NOVEL01.DOC and names it NOVEL01.BAK. The copy of the file is located within the same directory as the original.

Checklist

▼ You list two file names when you use the COPY command. The first file is the *source file*—the one you're copying from. The second file is the *copy* (also called the *destination*, just to make things a little more obscure).

▼ There's a space after COPY, and after the first file name. Nowhere else.

▼ When you name the copy, you must follow DOS regulations about valid file names. (Chapter 14 explains all the DOS rules for naming files.)

▼ If you don't include drive or path information in the filespecs, DOS makes the copy in the same directory.

▼ If you do include the drive and path information and you are copying to another directory, you don't have to type the file name. DOS will use the same file name.

▼ When DOS finishes copying the file, you see a message, such as `1 file(s) copied`.

Copying a File to a Different Drive or Directory

Most of the time, people copy files to a different disk drive. Why? Two words: backup security. If a disk goes bad, you lose all the files on it, including copies you've made to the same disk. It's a good idea to make lots of copies of very important files. Place them on two or three floppy disks that you keep in separate places. That way, when your 72-oz. Big Gulp of Coke gushes out over your desk, there's a chance that at least one copy will escape the flood.

To copy a file to another drive or directory, include filespec information in the destination file name, as in this example:

COPY NOVEL01.DOC A:NOVEL01.BAK

This command tells DOS, "Make a copy of the file NOVEL01.DOC, name the copy NOVEL01.BAK, and store it on the disk in drive A."

Checklist

▼ When you copy a file to a different drive or directory, you can use the same file name. However, it's a good idea to use a different name so that you don't lose track of which is the original and which is the copy.

▼ To copy a file that isn't in the current directory, include the filespec stuff in the first file name (the source file), as in this example:

COPY C:\DOCS\NOVEL01.DOC A:NOVEL01.BAK

CHAPTER 15

Copying a Group of Files

You can use DOS wild cards to copy a group of files. To copy all the files in the C:\DOCS directory to drive A, type **COPY C:\DOCS*.* A:** and press Enter.

To copy only the files with the name NOVEL01 (NOVEL01.DOC, NOVEL01.BAK, NOVEL01.BAD) to drive A, type **COPY NOVEL01.* A:** and press Enter.

To copy all the files with the extension YOU (including LOVE.YOU, HATE.YOU, and DANG.YOU) to drive A:, type **COPY *.YOU** and press Enter.

Moving Files

Sometimes it's nice to move files—change their current residence from one disk or directory to another.

If you have DOS 6, you can move files with the neat new MOVE command. To move JUNK.DOC to drive A, for example, type **MOVE JUNK.DOC A:** and press Enter.

Older versions of DOS don't have a MOVE command that lets you move files in one step. However, you can move files by copying them to the new location and then deleting them from the old location. Here's how you would move all the *.DOC files in a directory to a floppy disk:

1. Type **COPY *.DOC A:**.

This command makes a copy of all the DOC files and puts the copy on the disk in the A drive.

2. Type **DELETE** *.DOC.

This command deletes the DOC files from the current directory.

CAUTION

> Before you delete the files from the old location, check the
> new location to make sure that all the files were copied!

Renaming Files

After you get used to the 8-character limit on file names, you may decide
to rename some files. LETTER, MEMO, and REPORT aren't going to
cut it when you have several hundred letters, memos, and reports. To
rename files, DOS provides the appropriately named RENAME command. The following command renames JUNK.DOC with the new
name PRECIOUS.DOC:

    REN JUNK.DOC PRECIOUS.DOC

Checklist

▼ Note that the old name comes first, followed by the new name,
with a space between the two names.

▼ For those who prefer to use full names to nicknames, you can type
RENAME instead of **REN**.

▼ REN isn't a way of getting around DOS's file name restrictions.
The new name must also obey the rules.

CHAPTER 15

The Quest for the Missing File

Sooner or later, you'll exclaim, "Heck! I can't find my file! It was there yesterday!" Don't panic—yet. Chances are, the file *is* on the disk. Somewhere. You probably saved it to a different directory.

Try the following extremely clever DOS command, which tries to find files by matching the name you specify. The location of the file doesn't matter. If it's on the disk, this command will find it.

Let's assume you're looking for JUNK.DOC. To search your whole hard disk for any copies of JUNK.DOC, type **DIR C:\JUNK.DOC /s /b** and press Enter. DOS then lists each occurrence of the file, indicating the directory in which it was found.

TIP

Put those wild cards to work. DIR C:*.DOC /s /b will list all files with the extension DOC, wherever they might be found. DIR C:\JUNK.* /s /b will list all the JUNK files, no matter what extension you used.

Top Ten Ways to Make DOS More Fun

10. Create secret codes to disguise tasteless jokes in file names

9. Use UNDELETE to see if there are any files someone thought they'd better get rid of

8. Figure out ways to use keyboard to make sideways funny faces, like :) (happy), :((sad)

7. Pronounce DOS ("doss") incorrectly ("dose") to the delight of coworkers

I HATE PCs!

6. Set DOS manuals on fence for target practice with .45 sidearm

5. Give prize at office for the Most Destructive DOS Command

4. Fold, spindle, and mutilate old DOS disks to let off pent-up frustrations

3. Use PROMPT command to add message that speaks to your innermost fantasies, such as "What is Thy next command, Highness?"

2. Try to imagine how on earth Bill Gates (Microsoft's CEO) got so rich selling this DOS stuff

1. Try to imagine what you'd do with Bill Gates' money

CHAPTER 16

Managing Files with File Manager
(The Windows Way)

IN A NUTSHELL

- ▼ Start File Manager
- ▼ Display files and directories
- ▼ Select files
- ▼ Delete files
- ▼ Copy and move files
- ▼ Rename files
- ▼ Find a missing file
- ▼ Use File Manager to run programs
- ▼ Undelete a file
- ▼ Create a directory
- ▼ Remove a directory
- ▼ Exit File Manager

CHAPTER 16

W indows users are lucky. They can perform basic file maintenance operations using an easier way than those cryptic
DOS commands—they can do it the Windows way! (*File
maintenance* means taking care of your files—copying, moving, renam-
ing, deleting, and so on.) The key is *File Manager*, a utility program included with every copy of Microsoft Windows. If you're using Windows,
you'll want to learn how to manage your files with File Manager.

"I HATE THIS!"

You can't avoid DOS

Because Windows is based on DOS, you still need to understand basic DOS concepts, like all that vexing "directory"
business. (Flip to Chapter 14 for an explanation of
directories.)

The File Manager has lots of features, but this chapter resists the gnaw-
ing temptation to drown you in them. This chapter covers just the absolute, fundamental, can't-live-without file management procedures that
you'll use in File Manager. You'll find lots of useful information for doing
things like discovering what files are on a floppy disk, copying and moving files, and finding a file.

Taking a Look at File Manager

(Warm up your mouse)

To start File Manager, you begin in Program Manager (see Chapter 4).
Open the Main program group, and double-click on the File Manager
icon. (This icon looks like a two-drawer file unit, and is helpfully labeled
File Manager.)

After a good deal of disk-access business, you see File Manager on-screen. File Manager uses graphics to let you see what's on your disk. Take a look, for example, at the graphic rendition of the directory tree.

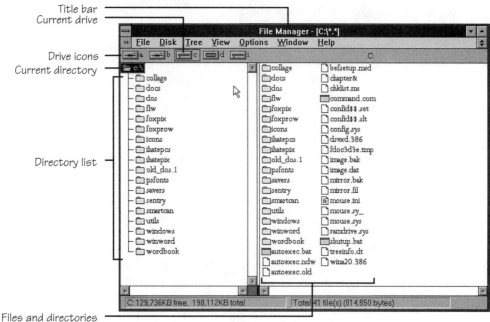

Title bar
Current drive

Drive icons
Current directory

Directory list

Files and directories
in current directory

▼ File Manager is a typical Windows application, which means that it has all the usual window stuff: the Control menu box, the title bar, the menu bar, the scroll bars, and all the rest. Chapter 4 provides thoughtful insight on these amenities.

continues

▼ You might find the window easier to read if you *maximize* it, if it isn't already. To do so, click on the Maximize icon in the upper right corner of the screen.

▼ The *title bar* lists the name of the current directory (probably C:\, the root directory). If someone previously used File Manager, you see the directory that was last displayed.

▼ When the drive window is maximized, there's one title bar. When the drive window is not maximized, you can move and resize it. This window will have its own title bar.

▼ Below the menu bar are the *drive icons*, which tell you the disk drives that are available on your computer. The current drive is highlighted with a little box around it.

▼ The window has two parts. The left part, called the *Directory Tree window*, shows the names of all the directories on your hard disk. Each directory is symbolized by a folder. (The open folder is the current directory.) The right part, the *Files List*, lists the files and directories that are contained in the current directory.

Displaying the Files Stored on a Floppy Disk

To display files that are stored on a floppy disk, insert a disk into the drive and point to the A or B drive icons at the top of screen; then click the left mouse button. Or hold down the Ctrl key, press A (drive A) or B (drive B), and release both keys. File Manager displays the files on the

disk that you indicate. You can then do things to these files—copy, move, delete, cut, clip, curl.

Change back to drive C by clicking on [C:] or pressing Ctrl+C.

"I HATE THIS!"

It says "Error Selecting Drive"!

If you didn't put a disk into the drive, there is a very long interval in which absolutely nothing happens. Finally, you get a stern alert box with a big exclamation point, which seems to say "Achtung!" This subtle reminder indicates that you forgot to put a disk into the drive. Put a disk into the drive and press Enter. The box disappears and the correct drive information appears on-screen.

CAUTION

If you remove a disk from one of the floppy disk drives and insert another disk, File Manager doesn't automatically update the Directory Tree or Files List for that drive. To refresh the list, press F5.

Displaying Directories

(The directory in the directory in the directory)

Think of directories as folders. You can store folders inside folders inside folders, and so on. You can't see any folders that are hiding inside other folders unless they've been opened, revealing their hidden contents.

I HATE PCs!

Checklist

▼ To see the directories within a directory, double-click on the directory folder. The listing opens (*expands*, in Windows talk) to show the next level of directories. The icon is now an open folder.

▼ To hide nested directories (called *collapsing a directory*), double-click on an open folder icon; the folder now becomes closed and the directories within the directories do a disappearing act.

Displaying Files

(What's in this folder?)

The Files List always displays the files that are in the current directory—the one with the open folder. But suppose that you want to display files in another directory. No problem. Just click on the directory name.

Checklist

▼ If the list of directories in the Directory Tree window is so long that you don't see the directory you want, click on the little down arrow on the right border of the Directory Tree panel. (If you go too far down the list, click on the little up arrow.)

▼ If you don't see the directory that you want, don't despair. The directory might be hidden within another directory. You need to expand the listing; the preceding section tells you how to perform this mystical task.

Selecting Files

To do something to a file, you first select the file in the Files List. A selected file appears in a different color (if you are lucky enough to have a color monitor) or in *reverse video* (black-on-white becomes white-on-black, and vice versa). You can select more than one file, which lets you do things to lots of files at once. After you've selected one or more files, they're sitting ducks for the things you want to do to them—like copy them, move them, or wipe them out.

Checklist

▼ To select a file by using the mouse, click on the file. The file's highlighted. That means it's selected.

▼ To select a group of files in a row, click on the first file. Then press and hold down the Shift key and click on the last file. All the files in between are selected.

▼ To select files that are not in a row, click on the first file you want to select. Then press and hold down the Ctrl key and click on the second file. Do this until you select all the files you want.

▼ To select all files, click on File in the menu bar; then click on Select Files. When the Select Files box appears, click on Select, and then click on Close.

▼ To deselect a file, click on another file. To deselect all files, click on File; then click on Select Files. When the Select Files box appears, click on Deselect. Then click on Close.

Deleting Files

After you have selected one or more files, it's easy to do things to them, like deleting, copying, tickling, tasting, or moving them. (Note, however, that the subjects of tickling and tasting files is beyond the scope of this book.) In this section, you learn how to delete files that you no longer need. (Of course, you will inevitably need them once you delete them, but that's beside the point.) Here's how:

1. Select the file or files you want to delete.

2. Press Del. You see a Delete dialog box. The computer suspects that you are about to do something foolish, and wants confirmation before proceeding with this rash act.

3. If you're really serious about going on, click on OK or just press Enter. If not, just click on Cancel or press Esc.

Checklist

▼ If you selected more than one file, you see a Confirm File Delete dialog box for each file. Choose Yes to delete the file, Yes to All to delete all the files, No to skip this file and continue, or Cancel to give up the whole idea.

▼ If you deleted the wrong file, use Undelete immediately, as described in the section "Undeleting Files" later in this chapter.

Copying and Moving Files

You copy files with the mouse by using something called *drag and drop*, which is what the cat does when it carts in those dead things. Hold down the left mouse button and, while you're still holding down the button, move the mouse across the surface of the desk. That's *dragging*. Then let go of the mouse button. That's *dropping*. You can do lots of file operations by dragging one or more files to something, like another disk or directory. This sounds a lot more complicated than it is.

Copying Files by Using the Mouse

This is how you use drag and drop to copy files:

1. Select one or more files in the Files List window.

2. Move the mouse pointer to the selected file's name (or names).

To copy the files to another drive, drag them to the drive icon [A:] or [B:]. To copy the files to another directory, hold down the Ctrl key and drag the files to that directory. You must hold down the Ctrl key. Otherwise, File Manager thinks that you want to move the files.

3. When you reach the drive or directory that you want to copy the files to, let go of the mouse button.

After you release the mouse button, you see a Confirm Mouse Operation dialog box. The computer demands to know whether you are really serious.

I HATE PCs!

4. If so, click on Yes. If not, click on No. If maybe, you'll have to just sit there, because there's no Maybe button.

Moving Files by Using the Mouse

To move files by using drag and drop, you use nearly the same set of steps, with one small twist:

1. Select one or more files in the Files List window.

2. Move the pointer to the selected file's name (or names). Press and hold down Alt, click and hold down the mouse button, and then drag to the drive icon that you want to move the files to (for example, [A:] or [B:]). You can also drag to another directory in the Directory Tree window.

3. When you reach the drive or directory to which you want to copy the files, release the mouse button and the Alt key.

   After you let go of the mouse button, you see a Confirm Mouse Operation dialog box. The computer demands to know whether you are really serious.

4. If so, click on Yes. If not, click on No. If maybe, throw the mouse to the ground and smash it to bits with your feet.

"I HATE THIS!"

Hey! That's my name!
If a file with the same name is in the disk or directory to which you're copying or moving the file, you see a warning box that asks you for confirmation. Unless you're sure that you

"I HATE THIS!"

know what you're doing, press Esc or click on No to cancel the operation. Why? Sometimes people unthinkingly give two different files the same name. If you proceed, you might overwrite a file that contains different data and if you do that, not even Undelete can get it back for you.

EXPERTS ONLY

Two, two, two windows in one

You can display two drives at once—one on the top, and one on the bottom—which makes it easier to keep track of what you're doing when you're copying or moving files.

To display two windows, double-click on the drive icon or choose New Window from the Window menu. In the new window that opens, click in the Directory Tree window to display the drive or directory that you want to see. Then choose Tile from the Window menu. File Manager arranges the windows in a totally cool way: one window on the top, and the other on the bottom. You can drag files to the other window and drop them there.

Renaming Files

If you don't pay close attention to file names, you may end up with file names such as LETTER1, LETTER2, LETTER3, LETTER4. Pretty soon—when you're frantically searching for that letter to the IRS—you'll realize that this isn't the best naming scheme. Fortunately, you aren't stuck with the file name you chose when you named the file; you can rename it. Here's how:

1. In the File List window, select the file you want to rename.

2. From the File menu, choose Rename. You see the Rename dialog box.

3. Type the new name in the To box, and then press Enter (or click on OK) to confirm your choice.

Finding a Missing File

Sooner or later, down the hall, you hear the keening lament of the computer user: "Heck! My file's gone! Oh, Darn!" (The language has been cleaned up so that we adults can imagine we are keeping younger readers in a prolonged state of naiveté.)

Chances are, the file isn't *really* gone. It was probably saved to some weird directory. (This is pretty easy to do. I have a directory called C:\WEIRD for precisely this purpose.) With File Manager, you can search your whole hard disk to find the file, and in all probability, it will turn up. Provided your luck is good that day.

Here's how to search your whole hard disk to find a missing file:

1. From the File menu, choose Search. You see the Search dialog box.

2. In the Search For box, type the name of the file you're trying to find. If you're trying to find JUNK.DOC, type **JUNK.DOC** (no spaces, please).

3. Press Tab to move the highlight to the next box, Start From. Then type **C:**.

4. Make sure there's an X in the little check box thing next to Search All Subdirectories. If there isn't, click on this box so that an X appears.

5. Choose OK.

If Search finds one or more files matching the name you typed, you see a Search Results window that lists these files.

▼ The file name includes all that path junk (like C:\DOCS\PROSE\TIMELESS.DOC) so that you can tell where the file is located.

▼ You can do stuff to the file—right in this Search Results window. All the commands on the File and other menus are available for doing stuff like copying, moving, or deleting the file. But you wouldn't want to delete it, would you? You just went to all this trouble to find it.

▼ If all you wanted to do was discover the file's location, just double-click on the window Control menu box (not the File Manager's Control menu box) to return to the File Manager. Be sure that you remember where that file was!

"I HATE THIS!"

It says "No matching files were found!"

Don't give up hope. Maybe you typed the extension or file name incorrectly when you saved the file, and it's really living somewhere on your hard disk under an assumed name. Try using wild cards in the Search For box (for example, JUNK.* will retrieve JUNK.DCC, JUNK.OCC, and JUNK.OC). For more information on wild cards (which work here just like they do in DOS), flip to Chapter 14.

I HATE PCs!

**Top Ten Destructive Acts Committed after File Loss
(followed by estimated average repair costs)**

10. Revolver emptied into computer screen ($409, not including $175 fine and 30 days for possession of unregistered firearm)

9. Attempted to connect computer to high-voltage circuit to "zap its brains out" ($1,487, not including loss of building due to fire)

8. Computer system unit struck repeatedly with baseball bat ($1,219, plus $16 for a new bat)

7. Computer system unit thrown through plate glass window ($2,676)

6. Local DOS guru thrown through plate glass window ($2.8 million, assuming out-of-court settlement)

5. Foreign object thrust into floppy disk drive (dry object, $95; food or other moist objects, $387; explosives, $1653)

4. Attempted to immerse computer's chips in Drano to "teach them a lesson" ($211, not including charge for emergency room care)

3. Fist through monitor ($13,421, including average medical care and disability)

2. Disk torn to pieces with bare hands and teeth ($0.62/disk)

1. Mouse thrown to ground and stomped to death ($72)

Running Programs by Using File Manager

You can also launch applications with File Manager. File Manager can launch an application that doesn't show up in Program Manager's group windows.

To launch an application, begin in the Directory Tree window. Select the directory that contains the application, and then move the pointer to the Files list and double-click on the application's file name. You can tell which files are applications: the file icon is a rectangle with a band across the top. (It's supposed to look like a window, get it?)

Undeleting Files

Sooner or later, you will accidentally delete a file that you need. A utility called Undelete can restore the file, provided that you use this utility *immediately* after performing the deletion. The restoration of a deleted file isn't a miracle; when you delete a file, DOS (which is lurking under Windows at all times) doesn't actually erase the file, it just removes its name from a file list that's stored on the disk. You can recover the file by putting the name back in DOS's list.

If you are using DOS 6, the latest version of DOS, you can use MWUNDELETE. (If you have Version 5 of DOS, flip to Chapter 14 to learn how to undelete files using the DOS version of Undelete. To access DOS, quit Windows by choosing Exit from the Program Manager's File menu.)

I HATE PCs!

"I HATE THIS!"

I've got an earlier version of DOS! What do I do?

If you don't have version 5 or 6 of DOS, stop working immediately and go get help from your local DOS wizard. Chances are, this resourceful person will have an industrial-strength undelete program that can recover your file. But it's really important that you *don't* use your system—if you do, your drive may overwrite the deleted file, and then it will be gone for good.

Here's how to use MWUNDELETE to undelete a file:

1. Press Alt+Tab to switch to Program Manager. (Hold down the Alt key and press Tab until you see the Program Manager title box; then release the Alt button.)

2. Open the Microsoft Tools program group window in the Program Manager. (This window was created by the DOS 6 Setup program when you or someone else installed DOS 6.)

You see Microsoft Undelete, with its big, funny buttons. (Hard to miss, aren't they?) Notice that Microsoft Undelete is displaying the deleted files for the current drive and directory.

3. Click on the Drive/Dir button, if necessary, to change to the drive or directory that contains the file you accidentally deleted.

After you click on this button, you see the Change Drive and Directory dialog box. You can type the directory name in the Change to Directory box, or you can click the drive or directory names in the Directories list box. (The [..] symbol refers to the parent directory, the one above the current directory. If you see this symbol, click on it until you see the names of all the directories in your

hard disk's root directory.) When you've typed or displayed the drive and directory you want in the Change to Directory box, click on OK or press Enter.

4. To undelete a file, highlight its name and click on the Undelete button. (If MWUNDELETE can't find any files to undelete, you see the message, `No deleted files found.`)

You see the Enter First Character dialog box. This dialog box asks you to supply the first letter of the file's name, which has been lost by DOS.

5. Type the letter; then click on OK or press Enter.

If MWUNDELETE is able to recover the file, the Condition column displays `Recovered`.

6. To exit MWUNDELETE, double-click on the Control menu box.

"I HATE THIS!"

It says, "File destroyed!"

Too bad. MWUNDELETE can't help you. Here's what happened. After you deleted the file, you performed other actions that caused your disk drive to write new information to the disk. This new information has overwritten the file you were trying to recover. It's too late, baby, now it's too late. Moral: Use MWUNDELETE *immediately* if you've deleted a file that you actually want to keep.

Creating a New Directory

It's a good idea to organize your data files into separate directories. You don't want your program and data files mingling. It's not kosher. Keeping all your data files in separate directories makes it easier to find and work with files.

Here's how you create a directory from File Manager:

1. In the Directory Tree window, click on the directory that you want to put the new directory in. If you want the new directory to be in the root directory, click on C:\.

2. From the File menu, choose Create Directory.

3. Type the name of the directory and click on OK. You can type up to 8 characters. It's a good idea to stick to characters and numbers only. Try to keep the name simple.

Checklist

▼ After you create a new directory, you can put stuff in it. See the earlier sections in this chapter for help on moving files.

▼ If you have no idea what a directory is, turn quickly to Chapter 14 and get the scoop.

Deleting a Directory

If you no longer need a directory, delete it to free up the disk space that the directory and its files take. If you need any of the files in the doomed

directory, first move them to a new directory. Then delete the directory. When you delete a directory, you also send all the files to the great beyond.

In the Directory Tree window, click on the directory you want to delete and press Delete. Windows displays a Delete dialog box, in essence saying, "Hey! You're gonna delete a directory. Are you sure?" Click on OK. Then, at the Confirm Directory Delete dialog box, click on Yes. If the directory contains files, Windows makes doubly sure you want to delete the directory. It goes through each file one by one and asks whether it's okay to delete the file. Click on Yes to delete that file. Click on Yes to All to delete all the files and the directory.

Exiting File Manager

To quit File Manager, just double-click on the File Manager window's Control menu box. (It's the one jammed all the way up in the upper left corner of the screen.) Voila! You see Program Manager again.

"I HATE THIS!"

That darned window won't close!

Be sure to double-click on the Control menu box for the File Manager window—not the Directory window. Double-clicking on the Control menu box for the Directory window closes that window, if you have more than one open. If you have just one Directory window open, double-clicking on it does nothing. You have to have at least one window open.

CHAPTER 17

Programs That Actually Do Things

IN A NUTSHELL

- ▼ What an application is
- ▼ The big three software applications
- ▼ Other cool programs you can use
- ▼ How to keep your system humming
- ▼ Using the computer to learn stuff
- ▼ How to have some fun
- ▼ What shareware is and why it's so cheap

Guess what? The point of using the computer *isn't* to refine your DOS or Windows skills. It's to actually do something *constructive*. (Imagine!) And to do something constructive, you need an application.

BUZZWORDS

APPLICATION

An *application* is the use of the computer for some creative or productive purpose, such as printing mailing labels, composing prize-winning poetry, or designing a community newsletter. An *application program*, then, is a computer program that helps you do one of these things. In common use, any single use or combination of these terms—*application, program, software*—works. Take your pick: application program, program, software program, software application, and so on.

The Big Three

The most common types of software are word processing programs, spreadsheet programs, and database programs. These programs computerize the most-often-performed tasks that people conventionally tackled on paper.

CAUTION

The biggest mistake people make with software is buying too many programs and getting overwhelmed. Most successful computer users run just two or three programs.

Word Processing Programs (The village wordsmith)

With word processing software, you can create, edit, format, and print all kinds of text documents. (*Formatting* refers to making the text look good on the page.) You can create memos, letters, resumes, newsletters, manuals, dissertations, books. If text is your thing, get a word processing program. Actually, even if it isn't your thing, you should have one. Lots of people who hate to write still have to crank out letters, memos, and reports, and word processing makes this wearisome task easier.

What makes word processors nifty

▼ Adding text with a word processor is easy. You just move the cursor to where you want the text and type away. As you're typing, you can press the Backspace key to correct mistakes as you go.

▼ To edit your text, you *select* the text using the mouse or keyboard. After you select text, you can *edit* it. You can delete it, copy it, or move it somewhere else. In this way, you can quickly restructure and rework a document without having to retype the whole thing.

▼ You can also format the text you've selected. You can change fonts (typefaces), font sizes, emphasis (like bold or italic), line spacing, alignment (right, left, or centered), and indents.

▼ As a finishing touch, you can add page formats, such as margins, page numbers, headers (those short titles that appear on every page), and even footnotes.

▼ Are you a lousy speller? A lousy typist? Most word processors have a speller program that will check your spelling. Although a speller can't catch all your errors (it won't flag you if you use *their* when you mean *there*), it will point out many of the problems.

▼ Can't find the right word? Lots of word processing programs come with a built-in thesaurus that helps you spice up your writing.

CHAPTER 17

Popular Word Processor Programs	
The Program	The Scoop
WordPerfect	A great, full-featured, if somewhat quirky word processing program. Dynamite for just about every word processing application, including office work (it even does mailing lists and mailing labels), legal documents (it's a whiz at referencing legal citations), and university dissertations (great footnotes). A plus: in any organization, lots of people know WordPerfect, so it's easy to get help. Available for DOS and Windows.
Microsoft Word	Another popular full-featured word processing program. Dearly beloved by scriptwriters because it handles those weird movie and TV script formats nicely. Available for DOS and Windows. The Windows version is currently the hottest-selling Windows word processing program.
Ami Pro	A Windows-only word processing program. It's great if you do a lot of fancy formatting.

Spreadsheet Programs (I've got your number)

A close second in popularity is the electronic spreadsheet program. The term *spreadsheet* refers to the lined worksheet that accountants use, and spreadsheet programs deal with numbers. You can create budgets, financial plans, and profit and loss statements. Spreadsheet programs may sound as if they are only for businesses, but you can also use them to balance your checkbook, figure your taxes, and perform a multitude of

264

other mundane number-crunching tasks. If you need to fiddle with figures, use a spreadsheet program.

Cool things about spreadsheets

▼ A spreadsheet program begins with a blank worksheet, which has rows and columns. Where a row and column intersect, you have a *cell*. A cell just looks like a small rectangle on-screen and is referred to by it's row and column—A2, for example.

▼ Now for the interesting part. In any blank cell, you can create *formulas* that calculate totals. You can type numbers directly into a formula, like this: **2+2**, but the hottest stuff happens when you type cell references (cell addresses), like **A2+A3**. After you finish typing the formula, you don't see the formula—you see the result. Let's say you put the formula A2+A3 in cell A4. If A2 contains 5, and A3 contains 10, Cell A4 would add these two numbers and display the result: 15.

▼ You can copy formulas across a row or down a column. When you do, the copied formulas automatically adjust so that they add up their own row (or column). Don't ask me how this works—just take it on faith.

▼ Spreadsheets aren't just for calculating a total. After you've typed in all those numbers and formulas, you can also plug in some new numbers "just to see what happens." This is called *what-if analysis* by those in the know. By typing a much larger number in the Net Income cell, you can fantasize about how much faster you'd be able to buy that beach condo.

▼ Most spreadsheet programs can make cool-looking graphs of the numbers you enter so that you can *see* that your entertainment budget makes up 44 percent of your income this month. Too much fun?

I HATE PCs!

Popular Spreadsheet Programs	
The Program	The Scoop
Lotus 1-2-3	The biggest-selling spreadsheet program—the standard. Like WordPerfect, a lot of people know Lotus, so it's easy to get help. Available for both DOS and Windows.
Excel	The best-selling Windows spreadsheet program. This program is a powerhouse, and is also easy to use. Has many features for advanced statistical and financial analysis.
Quattro Pro	A hot-selling rival to Lotus 1-2-3, this spreadsheet program sells for less—and claims to offer more—than 1-2-3. Available for DOS and Windows.

Database Programs

In third place, and not likely to zoom any further up the charts, are database management programs.

A *database management program* is essentially a computerized version of a library card catalog. In a library card catalog, each individual card is a data record; it holds one unit of information about one item—often a book. On the card are data fields, where certain types of information appear, such as the author's name and the title.

Nifty things about databases

▼ The basic unit of data storage is a data record. A *data record* contains information about one of the things you're tracking—one book, compact disk, employee, homing pigeon, or whatever. On the record are *data fields*, which contain specific information—Beak Type, Plumage Color, Last Seen, and the like.

▼ It's easy to edit and update the information. Suppose the homing pigeon named Bernard suddenly reappears. You display the record for Bernard, and type today's date in the Return Date field.

▼ You can sort the information in various ways. In seconds, you can sort your database by Pigeon's Name, Date Released, Plumage Color—anything you want.

▼ The best thing about database management programs is that you can analyze the stored data—essentially, by asking questions about it. This is called *querying*. For example, you could ask, "What is the average age of pigeons who survived the last release?" Or "What percentage of pigeons with speckled grey plumage returned within 5 days of release?" Just imagine the possibilities!

▼ You can print the information in your database. The printout is called a *report*.

Popular Database Programs

The Program	The Scoop
FoxPro	A fast and advanced, but very quirky and difficult, database management program with many advanced features. Not really for people who aren't into computer programming. Available for DOS and Windows.

continues

Popular Database Programs, continued	
The Program	**The Scoop**
dBASE	A big, complex database management program, but somewhat easier to use than FoxPro. Soon to be available for Windows.
Microsoft Access	A program that provides ordinary users like you and me a "friendly" way to get into data stored in big, nasty databases. A sizzling-hot seller.
FileMaker Pro	An easy-to-use but fairly advanced database. You can create impressive database applications without hiring a database developer. Available for Windows.
Paradox	Yet another big, complex database management program that tends to make nonprogrammers break into hives. Available in both DOS and Windows.

Beyond the Big Three

Besides the big three general applications—word processors, spreadsheets, and databases—there are hundreds and hundreds of other, more specialized programs. Many of these programs are designed to do stuff that you could do with one of the Big Three—if you're willing to spend days setting everything up. These programs do all that work for you.

This section gives you a sampling of programs that lots of people have found really useful. I haven't tried all these myself, but they're popular and widely available.

Other Programs

The Program	The Scoop
Address Book and Label Maker (Power Up Software)	Keeps a mailing list and prints mailing labels in over 40 formats; includes soft fonts for attractive printouts.
AutoMap (AutoMap)	A computerized atlas—sort of like having your own AAA office. Plans and prints the best route from Point A to Point B.
Calendar Creator Plus (Power Up Software)	Creates and prints calendars with appointments, prioritized to-do lists, and personal scheduling.
Harvard Graphics (Software Publishing Corporation)	Quickly prints groovy-looking charts and graphs for your next winning presentation. You can save them to a special format that can be made into colorful 35mm slides, if you really want to wow 'em.
It's Legal (Parsons Technology)	Lets you quickly generate binding legal documents such as wills, power of attorney letters, living trusts, and much more.
PowerPoint (Microsoft)	Incredibly easy-to-use presentation graphics. Just click and type to make stunning-looking presentations in minutes.

continues

I HATE PCs!

Other Programs, continued

The Program	The Scoop
Print Shop (Brøderbund)	Quickly prints greeting cards, newsletters, posters, and more.
Publish It! (Timeworks)	Easy-to-use desktop publishing program that includes 150 ready-to-use templates for newsletters, flyers, brochures, and more. (A *desktop publishing program* is designed to help you lay out text on the page for special-purpose publications, such as newsletters or brochures.)
QuickBooks (Intuit)	A simple accounting program for small businesses. Handles payroll, prints W-2s, and simplifies a variety of other accounting hassles. Wildly popular.
Quicken (Intuit)	Gets your checkbook, spending, and budget organized—finally. Lets you track each check you write, and code it by category. Produces great reports and graphs that show just where your money's going. Even enables you to write checks on-sceen and print them on bank-approved computer checks, which makes monthly bill-writing a breeze.
Turbo Tax (Chipsoft)	Walks you through the entire ordeal of doing your taxes, and prints the results on IRS-approved facsimiles of real tax forms.

The Program	The Scoop
Typing Tutor (Que Software)	Teaches you quickly how to type the ten-fingered way.
WealthBuilder (Reality Software)	*Money Magazine's* comprehensive solution for tracking and optimizing your investments and personal finances.

Top Ten Rejected Software Ideas

10. Generates numbers that "look right" for IRS Form 1040 and Schedule A

9. On-screen pop-up reminds you when *Gilligan's Island* is on

8. Tracks verified Elvis sightings; uses secret formula to predict location of next appearance

7. Figures out all possible Mr. Potato Head configurations

6. Suggests the best way to sort your laundry (based on your own personal list of dirty clothes) and indicates prime water-temperature settings

5. Creates fictitious but plausible genealogy demonstrating roots back to the *Mayflower*

4. Reads Rod McKuen poems to you

3. For worriers: from user-supplied data, automatically constructs worst-case scenarios for a variety of family, work, and health problems

continues

I HATE PCs!

CHAPTER 17

Top Ten Rejected Software Ideas, continued

2. Stores database of processed cheese-product recipes

1. Adds scenic pictures from hazardous waste dumps to your documents

System Utilities

(Keeping things hummin')

Think about the equipment it takes to keep your house looking nice. As long as you have the rock-bottom necessities—a good broom, a can of Black Flag, a couple of gallons of vinegar, a boar bristle brush, and bottle of Drano—you can solve any problem. In the same way, you need a few system utility programs to keep your computer system humming. These are extra programs that may or may not come with your computer. This section discusses the basic system utilities, and tells you why they're needed.

Back It Up (Or else...)

Fact 1: Very few people back up their work by copying it on to floppy disks or special backup tapes. Fact 2: All hard disks eventually die—and in many cases, you can't recover the files unless you have a backup. Fact 3: Many people fervently wish they *would have* backed up when a nasty hard disk crash wipes out several months of work. Cheerful prospect, isn't it?

BACK UP

To copy the data on your hard disk to a different place (a set of floppies, another hard drive, or a backup tape—a storage device designed just for backups). If your hard disk fails, not to worry—you've got a backup copy.

A *backup utility* is a program that copies files from your hard disk to floppy disks. You begin by backing up all the files on your whole disk. This is a tedious job and can involve as many as 50 or 100 floppy disks. After that, it's easier. The utility "knows" which files have been backed up, and which ones haven't, so subsequent backups involve only the files you have created or changed since the first backup. And if your disk fails, you need only reverse the backup process—in an operation called a *restore*—and presto! Your disk is restored, just the way it was at the time you last backed up.

The best backup utility programs are easy to use and copy the files at much higher speeds than DOS or Windows can. Popular backup utilities include Central Point Backup, Norton Utilities (Symantec), and Fastback Plus.

Doubling Your Disk Space (Squeeze those files!)

It's inevitable that your hard disk will soon be crammed with programs, files, more programs, and more files. Files seem to multiply at a furious pace. Sooner or later (probably sooner), you are going to run out of space on your hard disk. That's when a disk compression program comes in handy.

A *disk compression program* works by getting your disk into a full nelson and squeezing until the disk agrees to store your data more tightly than it normally would. Don't worry; it's safe. And provided that the disk complies, no one gets hurt.

Restoring Your Hard Disk's Peak Performance

You won't like what you're about to read, but it's true: DOS is likely to store your precious data here and there all over the hard disk, rather than putting it all in one nice, continuous unit. This phenomenon is called *file fragmentation* and makes your hard drive run more slowly. When you tell DOS you want a file, it has to run around the hard disk, frantically collecting all the pieces. This process can take some time.

The cure for file fragmentation is running a *defragmentation utility*, a program that rewrites all the data on your disk so that all the file parts are put back together. Disk defragmentation utilities are usually included in *utility packages* (collections of utility programs) such as Norton Utilities or PC Tools. DOS 6 comes with DEFRAG, a version of the Compress program included with PC Tools.

The Great Virus Hunt

What's a virus? Basically, a *virus* is a prank program designed to do something unexpected to your computer. Sometimes the unexpected is something silly such as displaying a `Bob Ross Lives!` message on-screen on a certain day at a certain time. More often the result is an annoyance—one virus makes your screen "melt" so that you can't see what you're doing. Sometimes the surprise is vicious; some viruses wipe out every last file on your hard disk, beyond recovery. One virus even set up a video pattern that was capable of setting fire to certain computer monitors.

Viruses are created by *hackers* (computer enthusiasts who enjoy making unauthorized modifications to programs and breaking security systems). Viruses propagate by traveling unseen on floppy disks. If you insert an infected disk into your system and start an infected program, the virus immediately infects as many of your files as it can. After infecting your system, many viruses operate for a long time without your being aware of their presence. During this time, you might give disks to others, who in turn infect their systems.

Your best defense against viruses is to run no program on your computer unless you've taken the program disks yourself from a fresh, shrink-wrapped package. Don't use programs from any other source.

To make sure your system is free from viruses, you might want to use an anti-virus utility program, such as Central Point Anti-Virus or Microsoft Anti-Virus (MSAV). MSAV is included with DOS 6.

Educational Software

The market is filled with tons of programs that help kids (and adults!) learn basic skills. This table offers just a sampling of these programs.

Educational Programs	
Program	The Scoop
Bodyworks (Software Marketing)	Examines human anatomy. For grades 4 and up.
Easy Street (Mindplay)	Take a shopping trip and learn basic economic literacy, like counting money and following directions. For children ages 4 through 8.
KidPix (Brøderbund)	Cool "paint" program that makes neat sounds as you draw—provided you have a sound board.
Math Blaster Plus (Davidson)	Great drill and practice game for addition, subtraction, division, fractions, decimals, and percents. Grades 3 through 6.

continues

I HATE PCs!

CHAPTER 17

Educational Programs, continued

Program	The Scoop
Reader Rabbit (Learning Co.)	Early reading game for first- and second-grade children.
Treasure Cove (Learning Co.)	Learn to identify sea creatures; teaches deductive reasoning, reading, and math, also. For ages 5 through 9.
Where in the USA is Carmen Sandiego? (Brøderbund)	Popular geography program that uses a fun mystery game approach. Also available: Where in the World is Carmen Sandiego? and Where in History is Carmen Sandiego? Grades 4 and above.

TIP

Parents, don't neglect CD-ROM if you're setting up a system for your kids. (If the word CD-ROM means nothing to you, take a look at Chapter 11, where this technology is explained.) A sampling of titles: *Macmillan Dictionary for Children, New Grolier Multimedia Encyclopedia, Software Toolworks World Atlas,* and *Where in the World is Carmen Sandiego?* (Deluxe Edition, with 130 digitized color photos, 150 recordings of traditional folk songs, and more than 3,000 clues.) Skip the Britannica and get a 486 computer with a CD-ROM drive.

Fun and Games

(Finally!)

This is what people *really* use computers for.

Fun and Games in the Computer World

The Program	The Scoop
A Train (Maxis)	You manage an urban transport network in a growing city. Keep the smog down!
Air Bucks (Impressions)	More interested in the economic side of aviation? Build a global airline empire from humble beginnings—one plane and one landing strip. Outfox your competition.
Design Your Own Railroad (Abracadabra)	Design and run your own model railroad without needing a lot of space. Excuse me, I'm going to order my own copy—back in 10 minutes.
Falcon (Spectrum Holobyte)	Step into the cockpit of an F-16. Your mission? Two words: Defend freedom.
Flight Simulator (Microsoft)	Pilot a Cessna 182 in this super-realistic simulation. Learn all the basics of flight, including takeoff, turns, landing, and even navigation. For diversion, take on the Red Baron.

continues

I HATE PCs!

Fun and Games in the Computer World, continued	
The Program	**The Scoop**
King's Quest VI (Sierra)	Latest installment in graphics adventure game. Rescue the princess in peril.
SimAnt (Maxis)	Your objective: Beat the red ants in a life-and-death struggle to take over the yard and drive the humans from the house.
Sports 3-Pak (Electronic Arts)	John Madden Football, Earl Weaver Baseball, and Lakers/Celtics come to life on your screen.

What's This "Shareware" Stuff?

Programs for $4 a disk? It couldn't be worth bothering with, could it? Well, maybe. *Shareware programs*, also called *user-supported programs*, are distributed by mail-order companies that sell the programs at ridiculously low prices. Here's the idea: you try the program on your computer, and if you like it, you send the program's author a registration fee. This might be as little as $10, although the typical fee ranges from $35 to $75.

Why is shareware so cheap? Low expenses. There's probably a rudimentary manual, at best, and no telephone technical assistance. The author hasn't spent a dime on promotion, advertising, distribution, transportation, dealer incentives, or the like.

CHAPTER 18

Installing and Running Programs
(Are We Having Fun Yet?)

IN A NUTSHELL

- ▼ Determine whether a program will run on your computer
- ▼ Install a new program
- ▼ What happens during installation
- ▼ Start a program
- ▼ Decide whether to upgrade to the latest version

That nice, new software package is sitting next to your computer, but there's one problem: the software's in the box, not in your computer. To use the program, you must *install* it—that is, copy the program from the floppy disks in the box to your computer's hard disk. Unfortunately, there's more. You will probably have to *configure* the program (which means telling it what kind of printer and video adapter you have), and other tedious stuff of that nature. And after all that's done, you get to test your work by trying to run the program—with any luck, it will pop up happily on-screen. This chapter covers the highlights of this entire process.

"Will It Run on My Computer?"

A good question, and one worth answering before you tear open the package. Look on the program's box for a section called "System Requirements." (This is almost always printed on the outside of the box—often on the back of the box.)

"I HATE THIS!"

Oops! I opened the box and I can't run the program

Most computer stores and mail-order outfits will let you return the program *if* you haven't opened the box. But if you rip open everything, including the little envelope that contains the disks, some stores won't take the program back, out of fear that you ordered it with the dishonest intention of copying the disks and then getting a refund.

Also, before you tear open the package, make sure that you get a program that has the correct size of floppy disks for your computer. Most programs are available in two versions, one with 5.25-inch and the other with 3.5-inch disks. If you have both drive sizes, don't worry.

"I HATE THIS!"

If you only have one drive size, check the box to find out whether you purchased the right size; the box usually says something like, "Includes 3.5-inch disks." What if you didn't get the right size? Take back the unopened package and exchange it for the version that contains the correct disk size. Otherwise, you'll have to write to the software publisher to get the disks in the other size, and on top of having to wait, they'll probably hit you up for 10 or 20 bucks.

What I Have

Before you can know whether a program will run on your computer, you need to know what kind of computer and software you have. Use this handy checklist. (This information will also come in handy when you are installing the program.)

My system has...

▼ My computer has version ___6.00___ of DOS. (If you're not sure what version you have, type **VER** at the DOS prompt, and then press Enter.)

▼ My computer has a ___486___ microprocessor. (8088, 8086, 80286, 80386, 80486)

▼ My computer has _____K of conventional (base) memory, and ___32736___MB of extended (XMS) memory. (If you're not sure how much memory you have and you're using DOS 5.0 or later, type **MEM** at the DOS prompt, and then press Enter.) *Hint:* All 386 and 486 computers come with at least 640K of conventional memory and 384K of extended memory.

continues

I HATE PCs!

My system has..., continued

▼ My computer has a __3·5__ floppy disk drive(s). (3.5-inch, 5.25-inch, both)

▼ My hard disk has _____MB of free disk space. (If you're not sure now much free disk space you have, type **DIR** at the DOS prompt, and then press Enter; look at the bytes free figure at the bottom of the directory list.)

36453248

▼ My computer has a __VGA__ display adapter. (CGA, MDA, HGA, EGA, VGA, or SVGA) *Hint:* If you're using DOS 5 or 6, you can type **MSD** at the DOS prompt, and then press Enter. The text next to the Video button tells you the kind of display adapter you have.

▼ My computer ~~does~~/doesn't have Microsoft Windows. (circle one)

▼ I have a color/~~monochrome~~ monitor. (circle one)

▼ My printer is made by ___CANON___. Its model name or number is __BJ 10Sx__. (Be sure that you include all numbers or Roman numerals, like DeskJet 500 or LaserJet IIsi.)

For a definition of all these terms, read the chapters in Part II of this book.

TIP

What I Need

Now compare what you have to what you need.

▼ If the systems requirement stuff reads "MS-DOS Version 2.11 or later," it is referring to the DOS version number. DOS 4 is later than DOS 3; DOS 6 is later than DOS 5. The requirement really should read, "MS-DOS Version 2.11 or any higher version number."

▼ The same goes with microprocessor numbers; you'll see something like "8088 or higher." 80286 is higher than 8088; 80386 is higher than 80286. If you're curious about these numbers and what they mean, flip back to Chapter 5.

▼ Does the program require Microsoft Windows? If so, you must have Windows installed on your system before you can even *install* this program, let alone run it.

▼ The systems requirement stuff might read, "5.25-inch or 3.5-inch low-density floppy disk drive." Don't let this one get to you. If you have high-density drives, they can read low-density disks just fine. If you're cloudy about the differences between a high-density and low-density floppy disk drive, take a look at Chapter 7, which explains a bit more about this subject.

▼ The memory requirement might read something like "512K of RAM required." This really means "512K or more." 512K is the absolute minimum you need to run this program. Chapter 6 explains more about the vexing and painful topic of memory.

▼ If you see a video adapter requirement such as "EGA color required," remember that this is another one of those *minimum* requirements. All video adapters are *downwardly compatible* with earlier adapters. This means that a VGA adapter can run software designed for CGA, HGA, MDA, or EGA adapters just fine. (Whew! What a lot of horrifying acronyms; if you're completely in the dark and craving a little illumination, go to Chapter 8.)

TIP

If you're installing a Windows application, consider that the minimum system requirements are often understated. If the requirement reads, "2MB extended memory required," for example, it means "This program will just barely run with 2MB." Double the figure if you want anything other than very snail-like speed.

Installing a Program with DOS

(Insert disk #27 and press any key when ready)

This section details the installation procedure for installing DOS programs. Skip this section if you're a Windows user.

TIP

If you're running Windows but want to install a DOS application (which is perfectly OK), quit Windows by choosing Exit Windows from the File menu in Program Manager. Then click on OK or press Enter to end the session.

Now you're ready. Note that the exact procedure varies from program to program, so be sure that you read the program's installation instructions. This is the *general* procedure that you follow to install a program:

1. Look for a disk labeled Setup or Install, and stick it into the floppy disk drive. If you can't find a Setup or Install disk, look for Disk #1, which probably contains the installation software.

2. Make the floppy drive *current*. To do so, type **A:** at the DOS prompt and press Enter to make drive A current. Or type **B:** and press Enter to make drive B current.

3. Look at the installation sheet or manual to find out what to type to start the installation program. You probably type **INSTALL** or **SETUP**. If there's no installation sheet or manual, look in the manual for a section titled "Installing Your Program," or something of that nature.

TIP

You can also do a directory of the disk. Type **DIR *.EXE** and press Enter. Most program files have the extension EXE; when you type this command, all files with the EXE extension are displayed on-screen. Look for a file named something similar to INSTALL or SETUP.

4. Type the installation command and press Enter. You'll probably type **INSTALL** or **SETUP**.

"I HATE THIS!"

There's no setup or install program!

If there isn't an automatic installation program, you'll have to wade into the manual to figure out how to install the program. Check the manual for the exact instructions and try to get a computer-savvy friend to help.

5. You are now in your computer's hands. You must do what you are told to do. You must sit attentively, waiting for screen messages, and attempting to answer all questions to the best of your ability, and as truthfully as possible. Hedging, little white lies, hesitation, or lack of complete faith in the computer will be electronically reported to the authorities.

I HATE PCs!

TIP

> If you see an option for a Quick, Express, Easy, First-Time, or Handy-Dandy All-in-One installation, choose it!

6. Eventually, you'll be told to remove and insert disks. Do so carefully, being sure the number on the disk you're inserting matches the number on the screen.

After a lengthy and grueling session of inserting and removing disks, you will finally see a message informing you that the installation is complete. You may be told to reboot (restart your system). If so, remove the disk from the drive, and then press Ctrl+Alt+Del or press the Reset button on the front of the system unit. Your computer restarts, and you see the good old DOS prompt again. (You might see Windows or the DOS Shell, depending on how your computer is set up.)

If you want to know more about installation, see the section "What Might Happen during Installation," later in this chapter.

Installing a Windows Application

This section details the installation procedure for installing a Windows application. Note that the exact procedure varies from application to application, so be sure that you read the application installation instructions. This is the *general* procedure that you follow to install a Windows application:

1. Look for a disk labeled Setup or Install, and stick it into the floppy disk drive. If you can't find a Setup or Install disk, look for Disk #1, which probably contains the installation software.

2. Exit any applications that might be running—only Program Manager should remain active.

3. In Program Manager, choose the File menu, and then choose Run. You see the Run dialog box.

4. In the Run dialog box, type **A:** (if your Install or Setup disk is in drive A) or **B:** (if your disk is in drive B), followed by the name of the installation program. If the program is called INSTALL, for example, type **A:INSTALL** or **B:INSTALL**.

5. You see an initial screen informing you that the installation program is copying stuff to your hard disk. After a while, things start to happen. You are now in your computer's hands. You must do what you are told to do. You must sit attentively, waiting for screen messages, and attempting to answer all questions to the best of your ability, and as truthfully as possible.

TIP

If you see an option for a Quick, Express, Easy, First-Time, or Handy-Dandy All-in-One installation, choose it!

6. Eventually, you'll be told to remove and insert disks. Do so carefully, being sure the number on the disk you're inserting matches the number on the screen.

After a lengthy and grueling session of inserting and removing disks, you finally see a message informing you that the installation is complete. You may be told to reboot (restart your system). If so, remove the disk from the drive, and then press Ctrl+Alt+Del or press the Reset button on the front of the computer. Your computer restarts.

What Might Happen during Installation

Chances are, all will go smoothly. Unless you don't have enough disk space for the installation. If you don't, you see a message and the

I HATE PCs!

installation utility just gives up. You'll need to move some files off your hard disk—or, better, get one of those disk compression programs discussed in Chapter 17.

▼ You'll probably be asked where you want to install your software. The program wants to know exactly where to place the program— that is, in which directory. The installation software might propose to make its own, new directory for the program. That's just fine. Let it.

▼ If the installation program doesn't propose a directory name, don't install the program in the root directory (C:\). You want to keep this directory uncluttered. When prompted to do so, type the name of a new directory. For instance, if you a installing WordPerfect, you might create a WP directory; you would type **C:\WP**. The installation program will probably create the directory for you.

▼ You may be subjected to a grueling list of questions, such as What printer are you using? What display adapter are you using? What was your mother's maiden name? Usually, you're shown a list of options, and can choose your printer or display adapter from this list. Use the arrow keys to scroll this list, if necessary. The installation program generally gives on-screen instructions for selecting printers and such, and often it is able to guess what kind of equipment you have.

▼ The installation program may ask you whether it's OK to modify your system configuration files (AUTOEXEC.BAT and CONFIG.SYS). Let it. What the heck?

Top Ten Least Popular Messages during Software Installation

10. Insufficient disk space; other applications removed

9. Virus found; adding virus code to original program disks

8. Not able to coexist peacefully with other applications; installation terminated

7. Plenty of disk space for multiple installation; installing 5 copies to fill all available space

6. Deleting system configuration files that conflict with application; press any key when ready

5. Installation completed (elapsed time: 4 hrs, 43 min); repeating whole process backward just for fun

4. Wrong disk inserted; restarting entire installation process from beginning. Insert Disk #1 and press any key when ready.

3. User configuration error; intelligent life form at keyboard not found, installation terminated

2. Choose a dominant screen scheme: M - Military Green, H - Hot Pink

1. Installation complete. Press Ctrl+Alt+Del and run for cover.

Starting the Program

(We're having some fun now)

After you've installed your program successfully, give it a whirl.

Starting a Program by Using DOS

If the installation program is worth its salt, you should be able to start the program from any directory, just by typing its file name and pressing Enter. (Leave off the EXE or COM extension.) Look in the program's manual to find out what to type. For example, to start WordPerfect, you type **WP** and press Enter.

"I HATE THIS!"

"I just installed SnazzyCalc, but it says 'Bad command or filename' when I try to start it!"

There are a couple of possibilities here. What are you supposed to type? It could be SNAZZY, SNAZ, SC, or even SZCLC. Check the program's manual, and try again. If it still doesn't work, you need help from your local DOS wizard. Chances are that the installation program is dumber than a tree and didn't add the necessary PATH statement to one of those weird DOS files in your root directory.

Ask your DOS wizard to add the necessary PATH command. In the meantime, you should be able to start your program by changing to the program's directory before typing the program's name.

Here are some common programs with the commands to start them:

Program	Command
WordPerfect	**WP**
Word	**WORD**
1-2-3	**123**
Quattro Pro	**Q**
Quicken	**Q**
dBASE	**DBASE**

Starting a Windows Program

The installation program probably created a new program group in Program Manager, and that's where you go to start the program. Open the program group (Chapter 4 tells you how), and double-click on the program's icon.

Should You Upgrade?

(New isn't necessarily better)

If you were a Good User and filled out your registration card, you'll probably get a notice informing you of a grand and glorious new version of

I HATE PCs!

the program. These new versions, called *upgrades*, fall into two categories: maintenance upgrades and major revisions.

Maintenance upgrades fix something that was wrong with the program or add a feature that some people really want, like an additional printer driver. If the upgrade fixes a *bug*, order it. If it provides new features, order the upgrade only if you really need it. (What's the use of ordering an upgrade if all it offers is a printer driver you don't need?)

BUZZWORDS

BUG

A *bug* is a problem with the way a program runs. The term originated back when computers were the size of rooms. One computer went awry and the technical gurus traced the problem to a huge moth stuck in one of the parts. True story.

Major revisions are new versions of the program, with major features added or drastically improved. These features are probably worth having; chances are they respond to the complaints users have been making, or offer features that competing programs already have. But it's up to you. No law dictates that you must upgrade.

"I HATE THIS!"

How can I tell the difference?

If the upgrade is numbered with a decimal increase, like Version 2.0 going to Version 2.1 (or 2.01, or 2.0001), it's a maintenance upgrade.

If the upgrade is numbered with a whole number increase, like Version 2.1 going to Version 3.0, it's a major revision. Easy enough.

PART IV

Help

Includes:

CHAPTER 19

It's Dead!

IN A NUTSHELL

▼ Get your computer started

▼ Deal with start-up error messages without resorting to violence

▼ Cope with the agony of sudden power outages

▼ Deal with system "crashes"

I HATE PCs!

Problems await every computer user, even the Technically Empowered. These are, after all, pretty complex machines. There's plenty of room for Murphy (of Murphy's Law fame) to wreak havoc, bringing annoyance, pain, and even devastation to the lives of millions of innocent computer users.

If your computer or program isn't running for some reason, this is the chapter for you. The next chapter deals with problems that arise after the computer (or the program) is up and running. You should also consult Chapter 21, which tells you how to determine whether you're up against something that will need to be fixed by an expert.

TIP

Don't traumatize yourself by spending hours trying to solve a problem. If you can't find the answer in a few minutes, get help. Flip to Chapter 21 for tips on getting the most out of your local DOS wizard, using technical support hotlines, and taking your computer to fix-it shops.

"I Can't Turn It On!"

It worked just fine yesterday, but today, you can't get your computer started. Chances are, you can solve the problem easily. Check the following:

▼ Is it plugged in? Is the power cord connected? Check the back of the computer. The power cord has two plugs, one on each end, and one of the ends has to be plugged into the back of the computer.

▼ Is the computer turned on? Locate the switch, and make sure that it's switched to 1 (which, to toolies, means On).

▼ Do you hear something? If the hard drive is going, maybe you just forgot to turn on the monitor. Locate the power switch, and make

sure that the monitor is turned on. And press a key or move the mouse to be sure that the screen isn't being dimmed by a screen saver program. Fiddle with the brightness and contrast controls on the monitor—someone might have turned them down. If the monitor's definitely dead, go directly to Chapter 21.

▼ Is the computer locked? Most computers these days have a funny round key that can be used to lock the system. To start the computer, you have to turn the key to the open position. Flip to Chapter 2 for the details.

▼ If you're using a *power strip* (one of those electrical things you can plug all your equipment into) or surge protector, make sure that the power switch is turned on. And make sure that the power supply center is plugged in. For more information on power strips see Chapter 2; for more about surge protectors, see Chapter 11.

▼ If the computer still doesn't work, unplug the power cord from the power strip or surge protector, and plug it directly into the wall socket. If the computer now works okay, the problem lies in the power strip or surge protector. Replace it.

▼ If even this clever maneuver doesn't work, make sure that wall socket is working. Plug something else into it, like a lamp, and see if it works. If there's no power, check the circuit supply box to see whether any of the circuit breakers have been thrown. Or, better yet, call an electrician.

▼ As a last-ditch measure, locate the circuit box in your house (a panel containing the circuit breakers for the circuit you're using), and see whether a circuit breaker has been thrown. (This is the modern equivalent of "blowing a fuse.") A thrown breaker switch is positioned in the middle, and usually has a little red flag that you can see behind a plastic window. Try switching on the circuit again, but call an electrician. If the breaker's thrown, something overloaded the line, and that could mean a short.

"I HATE THIS!"

> ## Worst Case Scenario 1: Dead Power Supply
> If some of the stuff (like the printer and monitor) comes on but your system unit shows no signs of life, and if you've checked the cords and power, your power supply may have gone bye-bye. Don't panic, this isn't a very expensive repair. See Chapter 21 to learn what to do now.

"It Started, but I See an Error Message"

If the computer starts, you're passed the first hurdle. But what if you see an error message and everything shuts down? Check the following:

▼ Is the keyboard plugged in? (It should be plugged into the back of the computer.) If it isn't, your system won't start, and you'll see a weird message that says something like `Keyboard error`. Turn off the computer and plug in the keyboard cable. Then try again.

▼ Do you see the message, `Non-system disk or disk error`? You left a floppy disk in drive A. Unlatch the drive, remove the disk, and press Ctrl+Alt+Del or press the Reset button on the front of the computer to restart your system.

▼ You start your system, and you see the message, `Starting MS-DOS...` but then, zip. Nada. Nothing. Zero. Chances are, you've made some changes to your CONFIG.SYS or AUTOEXEC.BAT files—did you change them yourself? Did you just install a program? Get your local DOS wizard to start your system by putting a floppy disk in drive A. Be sure to bring along some chocolate so that you can bribe this generous, wonderful person into taking a look at your system configuration files.

EXPERTS ONLY

Why drive A?

When your computer starts, it first tries to access drive A. This is because if your hard disk fails (horrors), you need some way to start your computer—so DOS lets you start from drive A and *assumes* that you'll be starting from this drive. Even with a bum hard drive, you can stick a disk into drive A, close the latch, restart your computer, and Lo! DOS loads from the floppy. You only need to do this if your hard disk fails, though. Under any other circumstances, make sure that drive A is unlatched when you start your computer. If DOS doesn't find a disk in drive A, it tries to start from drive C, which is what you want.

TIP

DOS 6 contains a new feature that lets you bypass messed-up configuration files. To use this feature, press F5 when you see the message, "MS-DOS is starting." This tells DOS to start your system with a *minimal configuration*. You can use the computer, although you may have to switch directories manually to start programs, and some programs may not run. You'll still need your DOS wizard to help you check out those configuration files, but in the meantime, you'll at least be able to *do* something.

"I HATE THIS!"

Worst Case Scenario 2: Your memory has gone bad

The computer starts, and things happen on-screen, but then you see a message during the memory check. This message says something like, "Parity error checking RAM," or "memory error," or even just some stupid number. This is bad news—one of those little chips that makes up your computer's internal memory (RAM) has gone bad. Write down whatever error message you get, especially any numbers. Then call in an expert for service, and see Chapter 21.

"I HATE THIS!"

Worst Case Scenario 3: Your hard disk has gone bad

When you try to start your computer, the memory test goes just fine, and there's no disk in drive A. But when your computer tries to access your hard disk, you see a truly horrifying message such as "Missing operating system" or "Invalid drive specification" or "Seek error reading Drive C." This isn't good news. Something's wrong with your hard disk—probably something unspeakable. Turn to Chapter 21, "When to Throw in the Towel." Hope you backed up your work.

"The Power Just Went Off!"

You're working with your computer, and everything's just fine. Except you hear a little thunder in the background. Aren't you glad you're inside, all nice and warm? But then the lights go out. The screen goes dead. The realization slowly dawns on you: You've lost your data.

I HATE PCs!

Checklist

▼ You've lost everything up to the time you last saved. Isn't that nice? That's why we computer book authors keep badgering you about saving repeatedly, preferably every 5 minutes. That way, you won't lose more than 5 minutes of work.

▼ When the power comes back on, your computer will restart, but you won't see your program. You'll see DOS, the DOS Shell, or Windows, depending on how your computer is set up.

▼ Restart your program. Then *immediately* try to reconstruct any work that you have lost—the longer you wait, the greater the chance that you'll forget. And make an immediate resolution to save your work more often.

▼ If you're living in an area where power outages are common, consider buying an uninterruptable power supply (UPS). See Chapter 11 for details.

"The Computer Won't Respond"

You type, you click, you swear, but there's no response; your program just stares at you, frozen on-screen. Is this a system crash? Hang? Freeze? Has it bombed? (Note that there are lots of picturesque synonyms for the same thing.)

▼ Try pressing Esc. You might be in some weird mode of the program that you're not familiar with. Try pressing F1 to get help. Try pressing F10 or Alt to activate the menu bar, if there is one. Try clicking your heels and chanting "There's no place like home." If any of these methods produce results of any sort, your system's okay.

▼ If you have a mouse, note that you might still be able to move the pointer around the screen even though the system is hung. Little parts of the computer are still alive—enough to move the pointer. If clicking the mouse does nothing, however, the system has crashed.

▼ Look at the *hard disk activity light* (the little light on the front of the computer). Is it blinking on or off? If it's off, you've got another indication that the system is hung. If it's blinking on and off, the program is probably carrying out some really lengthy operation; be patient. Control will probably soon return to the keyboard.

▼ If all else fails, press Ctrl+Alt+Del or press the Reset button on the face of your computer to restart your system. Unfortunately, you lose any work you haven't saved. (**Reminder:** Save your work, save your work, save your work.)

CAUTION

Even if you think your system has crashed, don't reset right away. When you reset the computer, you lose any work you haven't saved. If there's still a chance you're just stuck somewhere in a program you don't know very well, try getting some help from somebody who's knowledgeable about the program.

Top Ten Sources of User-Assisted Data Loss

10. Threw entire system out of third-story window after fifteenth `Abort, retry, fail?` message

9. Jarred power cord loose while attempting to affix Garfield doll to monitor

8. Inserted Guns n' Roses CD into floppy drive just to see what would happen

7. Told by "helpful" colleague that Ctrl+Alt+Del is the Save Data key combination

6. Thought the manual was serious when it read, "give it a boot," and that the computer had it coming, anyway

5. Kept working during thunderstorm, having mistaken distant booming sounds for Honor Guard drum roll celebrating return of boss to building

4. Struck Reset button accidentally during flamboyant mouse maneuver

3. Sprayed floppy disk drive with WD-40 in attempt to reduce those irritating clanking noises

2. Reformatted hard disk to try to free up a bit more disk space

1. Responded to `Drive not ready` message by shoving sandwich in drive door, and exclaiming, "Well, read this, pal!"

CHAPTER 20

Something's Wrong!

IN A NUTSHELL

▼ Get your program to start

▼ Get your mouse to work

▼ Fix the computer's time and date

▼ Deal with error messages when copying files

▼ Find a "missing" file

▼ Recover from accidentally reformatting a floppy or hard disk

▼ Handle error messages that you get while using a floppy disk

▼ Determine whether your hard disk is about to go bye-bye

▼ Make an obstinate printer print

This chapter discusses a whole series of minor annoyances that your system can occasion, as distinguished from the major disasters discussed in the previous and next chapter. Maddening and infuriating though they may be, most of these difficulties are solvable.

"My Program Won't Start!"

For months, you've been typing **WP** to start WordPerfect. Today you type it and see the message, `Bad command or file name`, if you're using DOS. (If you're using Windows, the Application Execution Error dialog box appears, informing you that apparently the Supreme Court has stayed the execution of your application.) What gives?

If you're a DOS user, did you just install a new program? The installation utility may have messed up your AUTOEXEC.BAT file, which would prevent you from starting your program. Get a DOS wizard to help you. You need a new PATH statement added to the AUTOEXEC.BAT file. (Your friendly local DOS wizard will know exactly what this is.) In the meantime, you can start your program by changing to the program's directory. If you're using WordPerfect 5.1, for example, the program probably lives in a directory called C:\WP51. To change to this directory, type **CD \WP51** and press Enter. For more information on directories, see Chapter 14.

If you're a Windows user, check the properties of your program icon. (The *properties* are a list of specifications about the program—like where it's located.) To see this list, highlight the offending program's icon and choose Properties from the File menu. (Alternatively, just press Alt+Enter.) You see the Program Item Properties dialog box. Check the Command Line box. Does it list the correct location of the program? If the program's location and name is C:\WP51\WP.EXE, and this box says something else, you've discovered why you can't start your program.

If you're not sure of the exact location or name of your program, you can click on the Browse button to see a File Manageresque directory tree and file list, which you can browse to locate your program. After you find the program, just double-click on the program's name, as if you were launching the application. Windows will place the correct filespec into the Command Line box. Click on OK to confirm. (If all this is sounds like gobbley-gook, get some Windows wizard to help you or consider a sister companion to this book, *I Hate Windows*.)

"I HATE THIS!"

Worst Case Scenario 1: You erased the program

Can't start the program after changing to its directory? Congratulations. You must have erased it or one of the "helper" files associated with the main program file. Or maybe the file has become corrupted, probably from reading cheap comic books. You'll need to reinstall the program. Chapter 18 covers this grueling process.

"Where's My Mouse?"

Don't expect your mouse to show up when the DOS prompt is visible; DOS doesn't do mice. But if the old, familiar mouse pointer doesn't show up where it should (in "mousable" DOS applications or Windows), something may have happened to the mouse driver.

A *mouse driver* is one of those system files that has to be left alone for your system to work correctly. It's probably called something like MOUSE.SYS, and this file must be correctly referenced in another system file, called CONFIG.SYS. Maybe you erased one of these files by accident, or maybe the file became corrupted. In any case, you'll need expert help. See the next chapter, "When to Throw in the Towel."

"The Time and Date Are Wrong!"

Almost all the computers sold these days have built-in clock/calendar circuits, which require a battery. The battery ensures that the circuits won't forget the time and date when you switch off the power. When you make a change to a file, DOS notes the date and time the file was last changed. This information can be important if you need to figure out which file is more current.

On some older computers, you have to type the date and time each time you start the computer. These computers don't have a battery.

If you're a DOS user, you can make sure that the date is correct by typing **DATE** and pressing Enter. You see something like this:

```
Current date is Mon 02-01-1993
Enter new date (mm-dd-yy):
```

If the date is just off a little, reset it. Type the date in the MM-DD-YY format, like **6/30/93**, or **3/2/94**; then press Enter.

To make sure that the time is correct, type **TIME** and press Enter. You see something like this:

```
Current time is 12:07:52.68p
Enter new time:
```

If the time is correct, just press Enter. If it isn't, type the time by typing the hour, a colon, the minutes, and **a** for AM or **p** for PM. For example, to set the time to 6:09 PM, type **6:09p** and press Enter.

If you're a Windows user, you can check the time and date by double-clicking on the Control Panel icon in the Main program group. When the Control Panel group appears, double-click on the Date/Time icon.

You see the Date & Time dialog box, displaying what the computer thinks is the current time. To change the date or time, click on what you want to change, and then just click on the little up or down arrows to raise or lower the number. Click on OK when you're done.

"I HATE THIS!"

Worst Case Scenario 2: The battery is dead

If the date is January 1, 1980, you've got a minor but irritating problem: your battery's dead. This minor inconvenience could become a major problem, however. Your computer's battery helps the computer remember what type of hard drive you have. If the battery goes completely dead, your computer forgets this information, and you may not be able to access your hard drive. Call for service; get that battery replaced immediately. And, while you're at it, ask the service person to reset the date and time.

TIP

To avoid having your work interrupted by a trip to the repair shop, have your computer's battery replaced every other year. They're supposed to last longer than two years, but don't bet on it. By the way, don't keep the spent battery around—it contains a deadly toxic chemical (cadmium). These batteries can kill—no exaggeration—if they're swallowed.

"I Can't Copy a File!"

This is a pretty common problem, and an easily solved one. Check these possible solutions:

▼ If you see the message, `File cannot be copied onto itself`, you tried to make a copy of the file in the same directory, and with the same name. (If you're using File Manager, you see the Error Copying File dialog box when you try to do this.) You can't copy a file to the same directory using the same name. It's an impossibility. It's also unnecessary. Copy the file with a different name, or copy the file to a different directory.

▼ If you're trying to copy the file to a floppy disk and you see the message, `Insufficient disk space`, you've run out of room on the floppy disk. Get a floppy disk with more room on it, and repeat the command; or remove some files on the floppy disk to make more room. File Manager users get the message `Destination drive full` that does something DOS does not: invites you to insert another disk to continue copying. Most agreeable.

▼ If you see the message `Write protect error writing drive A` or `Write protect error writing drive B` while trying to copy to a floppy disk, the disk has been write-protected, which means that you can't alter it. (Windows users see the message, `Cannot create or replace filename. Access denied. Make sure that the disk is not full or write-protected.`)If you need to unprotect the disk, flip to Chapter 7, which explains how to accomplish this feat.

▼ If you see the message `File not found`, use DIR to make sure that the source file (the one you're trying to copy) is really in the directory. Also, check your typing. You probably won't have this problem in File Manager, since you can't drag a file you can't click.

▼ If you see the message `Path not found`, DOS can't find the directory to which you want to copy the file. Check your typing. Again, this isn't a problem with File Manager.

▼ Chapter 15 tells you more about copying files with DOS, while Chapter 16 covers the same, tedious material for Windows users. Chapter 14 tells you more about directory names.

"My File's Gone!"

At one time or another, this phrase has been heard echoing through the halls of every company whose employees use a computer. The cry is generally followed by a string of obscenities, although the latter is optional.

Relax. Your file's probably on your disk...somewhere. Chances are good that you saved it to some weird place, like your root directory. DOS users, flip to Chapter 15 for information on hunting down the lost file; Windows users should flip to Chapter 16 for the same information in the Windows idiom.

If you think you might have deleted the file by accident, DOS users should immediately turn to the section "Recovering from an Accidental Deletion" in Chapter 15. Then run UNDELETE. (You must have DOS 5 or 6 to use UNDELETE. If you're using an earlier copy of DOS, stop what you're doing and go get a DOS wizard to help you.) Windows users, flip to the section "Undeleting Files" in Chapter 16.

"I Just Reformatted My Floppy Disk!"

I'm assuming here that you just reformatted a disk containing valuable data. Don't panic! If you're using DOS 5 or DOS 6, there's an easy solution. These versions of DOS perform a *safe format*, which means that you

can recover your data. The key to this wondrous capability is a DOS utility called UNFORMAT. But you must use UNFORMAT immediately, without doing anything else that would change the disk in any way.

To unformat a floppy disk in drive A, start from the DOS prompt and type **UNFORMAT A:**. Then press Enter. You see a lot of messages, and finally a confirmation request. Press Y to unformat your floppy disk. (You might have to press Y more than once.)

If you don't have DOS 5 or 6, don't do anything else with your computer. Go directly to your local computer wizard and ask for help. Do not pass Go. Do not collect $200.

"I Just Reformatted My Hard Disk!"

This takes some real effort on your part—you had to ignore DOS's repeated warnings that this is probably a dumb thing to do. If you're using DOS 5 or 6, you can recover your data. Just use the UNFORMAT program. To unformat your hard drive, start from the DOS prompt. Then type **UNFORMAT C:** and press Enter.

CAUTION

Don't try this "just to see how it works." You *could* lose some or all of the data on your hard disk. Use UNFORMAT on your hard disk only if you've just accidentally formatted your hard disk.

If you're using a version of DOS earlier than 5.0, don't touch your computer; don't even turn it off. Just let it be and go get help. Find your local DOS wizard, who will have an unformat utility program.

"This Floppy Isn't Working!"

You can tell, because you're getting error messages such as `Data error reading (or writing) Drive A`. In Windows, you get a pretty specific message, which even includes instructions on what to do. DOS users, you'll have to interpret the following, cryptic messages:

▼ If you see the message, `Not ready reading drive A. Abort, Retry, Fail?`, you probably forgot to put the disk into the drive or to close the drive latch. Close the latch, and press R for Retry.

▼ If you see the message `General failure reading (or writing) drive A`, DOS can't access the drive, but it doesn't know why. (That's why you see the "general failure" message; it's the DOS equivalent of the "little technical problem" that the cockpit crew tells you about after explaining that they're going to make an unscheduled landing.) Probably, you put an unformatted disk into the drive. Try another disk, or format this one.

▼ If you see the message, `Data error reading (or writing) drive A`, it's bad news—something's wrong with the surface of the disk. Immediately copy from this disk all the files that are still copiable, but don't use this disk again; either throw it away or use it as an office Frisbee.

"I HATE THIS!"

Worst Case Scenario 3: The file allocation table (What?) is bad

You may see the message "File allocation table bad drive A." This is really bad news—the table that keeps track of where files are located has been scrambled. See Chapter 21, "When to Throw in the Towel."

313

CHAPTER 20

"I Can't Access My Hard Disk!"

Hard disks, unlike diamonds, are not forever. You'll be fortunate if you get three or four years of continuous use. And when the end is near, you start getting little warning signs. Let's say you're trying to copy a file, and you get the message, `Read fault error reading Drive C`. You can't copy this file, but then again, other things work. But you start getting this, and other messages of the same sort, more often. These are pretty strong signs of impending disk death.

CAUTION

If you get lots of these error messages, the end is probably near. Back up your whole hard disk using a program such as MSBACKUP (DOS) or MWBACKUP (Windows), included with DOS 6. If you don't have DOS 6, get a backup program and do a full backup of your entire disk.

When you are sure you have successfully backed up all your data, have a DOS guru reformat your hard disk, and then reinstall a program or two. Try using the computer. If it works smoothly (no error messages), the problem had to do with the *surface* of the hard disk. You might be able to continue using it. To restore your data, see the next section.

If the disk still acts funny after you reformat it, forget it—you need a new drive. Do yourself a favor and get a bigger one.

EXPERTS ONLY

I have to use my backup data. How?

If you've been forced to reformat or replace your hard disk, you can restore your data from the backup disks. The type of backup program you used determines what restore procedure you need to use. For help restoring the files, see the manual for your backup program.

"My Printer Won't Print!"

Lots of likely causes here; most of them aren't serious.

Checklist

▼ Is the printer plugged in? Is the power on?

▼ Is the cable connected at both ends (computer and printer)? Check both connections to make sure they're tight and secure.

▼ Is the printer selected or on-line? There's usually an indicator light with a little button. If it's off, press the button so that the light is on, and try again.

▼ Is there paper? If not, load some.

▼ Is the paper jammed? Laser printers display a warning light when the paper's jammed. Clear the obstruction and try again.

"I HATE THIS!"

Worst Case Scenario 4: The printer isn't installed correctly

Is this the first time you've tried printing with a program? If so, maybe you didn't select the printer when you installed it. Get somebody to help you determine which printer is the current printer for this program. If it's listed incorrectly, change it. (You may have to reinstall the program to do so; Chapter 18 tells you all about this agonizing process.)

Top Ten Computer Versions of Murphy's Law

10. All really serious computer failures occur when the technical support hotline and computer repair shop are closed

9. The application that proves to be most useful will be the one most likely to cause work-destroying crashes

8. The disk you need isn't here (*Corollary:* The disks that are here will be useless)

7. The more you back up, the less likely that a catastrophic disk failure will occur

6. The less you back up, the more likely that a catastrophic disk failure will occur

5. A printer fails just when the most critical document is due

4. The one program feature you can't figure out is the one not discussed in the manuals

3. The DOS wizard who knows how to fix this is in Bermuda this week

2. Something that isn't working right will work just fine when the technician comes to check out your system

1. The more time you spend trying to solve a computer problem, the less likely you will succeed

CHAPTER 21

Getting Help

IN A NUTSHELL

- ▼ Try some last-minute tricks that might get it going
- ▼ Decide whether you're over your head and need help
- ▼ Describe your system to technical support and repair people
- ▼ Call technical support
- ▼ Get your system repaired

I t's not a happy sight when a computer dies. You hear the violin playing in the background as our hero gasps his last: "Parity error checking RAM." Actually, a real computer death is often over a lot more quickly. Suddenly, the screen goes blank or you see a funny interference pattern. Granted, computer demises are rare, but they do happen. And when they do, no amount of user finagling can get the computer going again. It's time to throw in the towel and get expert help.

Try These Tricks before Hitting the Panic Button

Computers heave a lot of information around, and even a tiny error can throw off the system. Try these tricks, known to computer cognoscenti but rarely communicated to beginners:

▼ If possible, save all your work and restart your system. Because this process enters fresh, correct copies of your programs into the computer's memory, this procedure will probably solve the problem.

▼ If you trace the problem to a particular program, try reinstalling the program from the original program disks. Once in a while, this trick fixes the problem.

▼ Unless you've been swapping programs with lots of people, the chances are slim that the problem's caused by a computer virus. But, you may want to run an anti-virus utility to make sure. See Chapter 17 for more information. (**Note:** An anti-virus utility comes with Version 6 of DOS.)

TIP

Those tiny little electronic components inside your computer are likely to fail when they're very young (less than three months old) or very elderly (more than five years old). If you're going to have a major hardware problem, it will probably happen when your computer is brand new or decrepit—not in between. If your system has been working for six months or a year, the chances are pretty good that the problem lies in the software, not the hardware.

Are You in over Your Head?

Computer problems can be really frustrating. And, there are lots of problems users can't solve on their own. Ask yourself the following questions:

▼ Have I spent more than 30 minutes trying to solve this problem?

▼ Is the computer still dead after I make sure it's getting power?

▼ Does the system crash every time I start or restart it?

▼ Is the system more than two years old? (If so, the battery may be dead.)

▼ Do lots of error messages appear when the system starts?

▼ Could I have accidentally erased some files in the hard disk's root directory (C:\)?

▼ Am I unable to access my hard disk?

▼ Did the problem start right after I installed a new program?

Answering "yes" to any of these questions is good grounds for getting expert help. Your next step is communicating to the expert what kind of system you have.

TIP

Your first recourse for help is your local DOS wizard, or any other knowledgeable user that you can drag into your office. Even if such people aren't able to solve the problem, they can probably narrow it down so that you can describe the problem more accurately to technical support or repair people.

Describing Your System

If something is wrong with your system and you turn to an expert, he or she might ask you to describe the system. Use the following checklist to fill out as much information about your system as you can. You need to know the following information:

TIP

If you're using DOS 5 or 6, you can use Microsoft System Diagnostics to get most of the information on this list. To use this program, type **MSD** at the DOS prompt and press Enter. You see a screen listing your system's current configuration. If you don't have DOS 5 or 6, check your system's manuals and sales receipts, or call the store that sold you the computer.

▼ Brand name _PHOENIX_

▼ Model number _A486 VERSION 1.01.E_

▼ Microprocessor (286, 386SX, 486DX, et al) _486 SX_

▼ Math coprocessor (if any) _NONE._

▼ DOS version _6_

▼ Total amount of RAM _640K (EXT 3328K)_

▼ Hard disk brand name and model number _CMOS TYPE 46_

▼ Total hard disk space _161 M._

▼ Video adapter type (MDA, VGA, SVGA, et al) _VGA_

▼ Mouse brand name _MICROSOFT._

▼ Type of mouse (serial, bus) _IBM PS/2 STYLE MOUSE._

▼ Mouse software version _8·20_

▼ Software version number (if it's a software problem) _____

Describing the Problem

("It's making a funny noise...")

Remember the look on the auto repairman's face when you said, "Well, it's kind of like a funny 'clank, gronch, bing' noise that I hear when I turn the wheel to the left"? The more you can pinpoint and accurately describe the problem, the better the chance that a technician will solve the problem.

I HATE PCs!

▼ Try to narrow down the problem so you can describe it to the person you're asking help from. "It isn't working" is hardly descriptive. Just *what* isn't working? The printer? The monitor? The mouse? Eliminate parts of the system that seem to be working fine until you've identified the problem component.

▼ Jot down any error messages you see on-screen.

▼ If possible, learn how to *reproduce* the problem. (For example, you might get a certain error message every time you try to print.) Then describe exactly what happens.

Calling the Technical Support Hotline

(Help!)

Computer companies and software publishers spend a lot of money maintaining their technical support hotlines. Probably, they'd prefer that I tell you, "Check the manual before calling technical support." But, very few manuals include a troubleshooting section that details solutions to common problems. You can check the manuals if you like, but I'll bet you don't find the information you need. Until better manuals come along, you're stuck with telephone help. (Or, you could purchase big, expensive books from Que Corporation—the publishers of this book.)

▼ Try to call first thing in the morning. Most technical support hotlines are busy, busy, busy, and you might be placed on hold for up to an hour if you call during busy times.

▼ Keep your computer manuals, disks, and receipts handy in case the technician demands to know your serial numbers. This is sometimes done to make sure you're a bona-fide, registered owner of the product.

▼ You'll probably have to negotiate a voice mail system. You may be asked to leave your name, telephone number, and a description of the problem. Leave this information. Most technical support people *will* get back with you.

▼ If you finally get a real, live human, you'll be asked to supply information about your system or the software that's giving you fits.

▼ Describe the problem in detail. If possible, reproduce it while you're talking to the technical support person so you can give a blow-by-blow account.

▼ Be nice. Technical support people often are treated as easy targets for the frustrations and rages of upset users. Keep calm. Keep in mind that your problem wasn't caused by the person on the other end of the phone. Those people are nice, real human beings, with names like Debbie or Jeff; at home they have cute pets and children. Don't dump on them.

▼ If you're told something vague like, "Oh, you'll need to modify your system configuration files," ask for specifics. What exactly should you do? And write down carefully what you're told.

Getting Your System Repaired

So it's a hardware problem, after all. This happens.

▼ Is your system still on warranty? Find out how to get it serviced. Some computer firms sell their computers with vague promises of "on-site" service, which turns out to be valid only if you are located within one block of the firm's Hope, Arkansas, headquarters.

▼ You may have to pack the thing off, UPS. If so, use the original boxes all that junk came in. (You did save them, didn't you?)

▼ Don't send anything back to a manufacturer without having obtained a "return authorization number" from the company. They might just bounce it right back to you.

▼ Did your system fail within 30 days of a "no questions asked" return policy? Consider returning the system instead of fussing with getting it repaired. Call for a return authorization number before sending the system packing.

▼ Not on warranty? Shop around for good repair prices. Beware of prices quoted at computer stores—they tend to be absurdly high. Check out the local garage operations; they can fix your system cheaply just by replacing the offending part, which is actually a better idea than trying to repair it.

▼ Ask the computer repair shop what you should bring with you: cables, software, monitor, keyboard, printer?

▼ Insist on a warranty for all the repair work that's done on your system.

PART V

Quick & Dirty Dozens

Includes:

I HATE PCs
Quick 'n Dirty Dozens

IN A NUTSHELL

▼ 12 Minor but Embarrassing Beginner's Boo-Boos

▼ 12 Good Things You Should Always Do

▼ 12 Acronyms People Expect You to Know

▼ 12 Most Common DOS Error Messages

▼ 12 Stupid (but Fun) Things to Do with Your Computer

▼ 12 Reasons to Upgrade Your Hardware

12 Minor but Embarrassing Beginner's Boo-Boos

1. **Leaving a disk in drive A when you shut down the system.**

When you start or reboot your computer, it goes a-hunting for DOS. First, it looks on drive A. And if it finds a floppy disk there, it tries to read DOS from the floppy disk. But, DOS isn't on this disk. And so you get that inspiring message, `Non-system disk or disk error`.

When you see this message, remove the disk and press any key to restart your system.

2. **tYPING wITH cAPS lOCK oN.**

The Caps Lock key is one of those irritating toggle keys. When you press it once, you engage the Caps Lock mode. This is sort of like a typewriter's Caps Lock key, in that the letters you type are in uppercase. But just to be different, any letters you type with the Shift key depressed are in *lowercase*, resulting in a strange pattern of capitalization unique to the computer world. Press the Caps Lock key again to turn off Caps Lock.

3. **Dumping your coffee into the keyboard.**

Sooner or later, it will happen to you. Believe it or not, most keyboards can take an inundation of this sort—if you remedy the problem immediately. Save your work, if you can, and turn off the computer. Disconnect the keyboard. Over a pile of newspapers, turn the keyboard upside down and burp it gently. Coffee will fall like rain from the keys.

Put the keyboard face down on a pile of tissues, and let it dry out. When it's dry, spray 409 or Windex onto a paper towel (don't spray directly on the keyboard), and carefully clean off the coffee stains.

4. **Inserting 5.25-inch disks the wrong way.**

There are a total of eight possible ways you can insert a 5.25-inch disk into a disk drive, but as you've no doubt discovered, only one of them is correct.

To insert a 5.25-inch disk correctly, make sure that the disk's label is on the side of the disk that's facing up. Now rotate the disk (without flipping it upside down) until the text on the label is upside down, from your perspective. The business end of the disk—the hole that shows the disk's surface—should be facing *away* from you. The label should be closest to you. Put the disk into the drive. Close the latch on the floppy disk drive. Then just recite the following ancient Vedic *mantra*, and you should be fine: "Ah-oh-eh-DAHS-ah."

5. **Inserting disks between the drives.**

This happens more often than you'd think. To remove the disk, you may need tweezers. If you can't reach the disk, get your local DOS wizard to remove the computer's case.

6. **Mispronouncing computer terms everyone else seems to know.**

A quick pronunciation guide:

386	Three eighty six (not "Three hundred eighty six")
ASCII	Ask-ee
CPU	See-pea-you

I HATE PCs!

DOS	Dahss, as in "floss" (not "dose")
GUI	Gooey (no lie)
KHz	Kilohertz
KB	Kay-bee, like that neat toy store at the mall. You ought to see the latest Lego Technic sets they have.
MB	Meh-guh bite
MS-DOS	Em-ess dahs (not "Ms. DOS")
RAM	Ram, as in "Spam" (not "arr-ay-emm")
user	Rhymes with "loser." Is that an omen? Northeast of New Jersey, and intensifying in Boston, however, this is pronounced "use-ah," thus rhyming with "vigor" (vig-ah).
VGA	Vee-gee-ay
WYSIWYG	Whiz-eee-whig. Is this the dumbest acronym you've ever seen, or what?

7. Logging onto the wrong drive or directory.

When you change drives, you log onto the drive you indicated. From that point, DOS assumes that you want your commands carried out on that drive, unless you specifically tell it otherwise. Let's say you are logged onto drive A, and you want to delete the file JUNK.DOC. You type the following:

    DEL JUNK.DOC

But you get the message, `File not found`. Should you assume that JUNK.DOC doesn't exist? By no means! You're simply logged onto the wrong drive. JUNK.DOC is on drive C, in the directory called C:\DOCS\TRASH.

You've two options. You can override the default disk or directory by including all that nasty path information in the command. Or you can switch to drive C, by typing **C:** and pressing Enter, and then change to the directory.

8. **Thinking your computer has crashed when it really hasn't.**

This is pretty common. Possibilities:

▼ You hit the Num Lock accidentally. Now you're trying to move the cursor but all you get are weird numbers. Just press the Num Lock key again.

▼ You forgot to turn on the computer or the monitor.

▼ You didn't close the latch on the drive door (5.25-inch disks only).

▼ You're using a new program and you've gotten into something you can't get out of. Try pressing Esc, Alt+F4, Ctrl+F4, Ctrl+C, Ctrl+Break, or F1.

▼ You're using DOS but you pressed the Esc key. The DOS prompt is gone and all you see is a funny little slash mark. This is OK; DOS is waiting for you to type another command.

▼ The mouse or keyboard cable came loose.

▼ The program you're using is taking its own sweet time to do something. Give it a chance.

9. **Buying software that turns out to be useless.**

There's only one kind of program worth buying: the one that's right for your needs. Unfortunately, it's not very easy to determine your needs, and it's even harder to get salespeople to understand them. But give it a shot. If you need to print mailing labels, ask yourself questions like this: "Self, how many people are on my mailing list? Do I want the labels to look really cool, with neat fonts and stuff? Do I want to sort the mailing labels by ZIP code (so that I can save money on postage)? Do I want to record other information besides name and address?" The better you're able to summarize your needs, the better the chance you'll buy a useful program.

Also, be sure that you get a program that your computer can run. Chapter 18 provides clues on decoding the requirement list you find on software boxes. Read the requirements before you tear off the cellophane.

10. **Starting Program Manager and then getting upset because you can't find Windows.**

Program Manager *is* Windows—at least, the part of it that helps you launch programs.

11. **Using your computer with the monitor facing a big, bright window.**

You could go blind doing this. The glare from the window makes it close to impossible to see what's on-screen. You can get an accessory called a *non-glare filter*, but it's best to move your computer so that the glare goes away.

12. **Not backing up.**

OK, OK, I know, you've already had this lecture. But you can really get into trouble by not backing up. Right now, it's a minor boo-boo—but it could turn into a major catastrophe. *Back up your work.*

12 Good Things You Should Always Do

1. **Save, save, and save some more.**

When you are working with an application, your work is in the computer's memory. It's *volatile*. If the power goes to lunch, so does your work. To be on the safe side, save your work every five minutes.

2. **Keep your UNINSTALL disk safe.**

When you or someone else installed DOS 5 or 6 on your system, the DOS SETUP program created something called an UNINSTALL disk. This disk is really important. In the event of a serious hard disk problem, this disk could hold the key to regaining access to all the data on your hard disk. Keep it safe.

3. **Keep your distance from the monitor.**

The jury's still out about the health effects of the low-level electro-magnetic radiation (EMR) produced by computer monitors, but why take chances? A careful study by *PC Magazine* indicates that the level of this radiation falls off to undetectable levels about 28 inches from the screen. If you keep your face and body that far away from the screen's surface, you've eliminated the risk.

4. **Protect yourself from repetitive strain injury.**

Repetitive strain injuries (RSI) represent one of the fastest-growing causes of occupational disability, and computers are clearly to blame. Sitting at the keyboard all day, performing the same hand and wrist movements over and over again, can contribute to RSI maladies such as carpal tunnel syndrome, an injury to the nerves of the wrist caused by scar tissue forming in a narrow bone channel.

RSI injuries can be extremely painful and disabling. To reduce your chance of injuring yourself while using the computer, follow these guidelines:

▼ Make sure that your keyboard is positioned at the level of your elbows so that you don't have to hold your forearms up to peck at those keys.

▼ Get a *wrist rest*. This is a pad that sits in front of your computer and takes the strain off your arms and wrists.

▼ Don't work more than two hours without taking a break.

5. **Win prizes!**

The registration cards that come packaged with software are valuable to you. When a new version of the program comes out, registered users can order the upgrade at a bargain-basement price, compared to what new buyers will have to fork over. You will also get notices of *maintenance upgrades*—minor revisions that fix annoying bugs or add certain new features—which may be of great value to you.

6. **Do your housekeeping.**

Spend some time organizing your hard disk; don't just add files and programs willy-nilly. Most important of all, create directories for your data files so that they're not mixed up with your program files. And periodically go through your files; delete the ones you're done with and don't need, and move the other ones to floppy disks.

7. **Label backup disks clearly.**

When you back up your work, be sure to write "BACKUP DISK" in big, bold letters. Also write today's date, as well as the names of the files contained on the disk. Keep your backup disks up high somewhere, far from coffee and Pepsi inundations.

8. **Learn to archive.**

There's another angle on backing up, called *archiving*. Here's the difference between backing up and archiving. When you back up your disk, you create an up-to-date backup copy of your disk as it is now, including all the files you're currently working with. If your disk fails, you can restore these files—that's why you back up. When you archive a file, you just move a finished file, one you're done with, off your hard disk to a floppy, and put it away. You're finished with it. You've printed it. You gave the report to your boss. Your boss turned it down. You don't need it on your hard disk. You probably wouldn't miss it if your disk failed. But who knows? Better archive it to make sure.

9. **Out with the old! In with the new!**

That big, behemoth program is taking up 12MB of disk space, and what are you getting out of it? Nada. Zip. Zero. If you don't use a program, archive any data files you created, and delete the program from your hard disk. (If you later change your mind, you still have the original program disks, so you can reinstall it.)

10. **Keep your root clean.**

Your root directory (C:\) should contain nothing but the files DOS placed there when you installed the program, together with the names of the directories created by installation programs and by you. If you add too many files to the root directory, your hard disk's performance degrades.

11. **If at first you don't succeed, look it up.**

I've seen a lot of beginning users just sitting at the computer for hours trying to get something to work. Believe me, it's not worth it. Chances are pretty good that there's just one little thing you don't know, or you forgot, and no matter how you try, you're just not

going to get anywhere. If you run into a wall like this, don't torture yourself. Get help. Look in this book. Get your local computer wizard to stop by. Ask coworkers. Call technical support. Flag down the paper boy. Do *something*.

12. **Don't take any of this too seriously.**

Computers are nothing more than useful tools for our work and play. At their best, they are wonderful tools for creativity, expression, and professionalism. At their worst, they are so maddening that they can send us into an infantile rage. Whether fair or foul, though, computers are pretty near the bottom of any reasonable list of what's important in life. If the computer starts getting to you, take a break, go for a walk, breathe some fresh air, take a look at the birds and the flowers. And then get someone to help you over whatever ridiculous roadblock the computer's thrown in your way.

12 Acronyms People Expect You to Know

1. ASCII

This is short for *American Standard Code for Information Interchange*. Basically, it's a set of numerical codes that corresponds to the standard keys on a computer keyboard. An ASCII file contains nothing but the standard ASCII text characters—no fancy extra stuff, like the junk that programs add to deal with extras like boldface or page numbers.

2. DOS

Yes, DOS is itself an acronym; it stands for *Disk Operating System*. Back in the early days, DOS was only that—a program used to control these fancy new disk drives (which, believe it or not, were once a novelty). DOS is more than that now, but the name has stuck.

3. GUI

Acronym for *Graphical User Interface*, and pronounced "gooey." An *interface* is the part of the program that communicates with the user. DOS, for example, uses a command-line interface, which means that you type commands and the computer fights back with error messages. This isn't considered very friendly, so computer designers came up with this GUI stuff.

In a GUI interface, the screen is filled up with colorful boxes and little pictures called *icons*. The pictures represent computer items or procedures, like disks or printers. You can use the mouse to move stuff around on-screen and to initiate computer operations by clicking on the icons. Microsoft Windows is a perfect example of a GUI.

4. KB (or just K)

You'll frequently run into KB when people are talking about file sizes or disk capacities. It's short for *Kilobyte*. The *kilo* part means *one thousand*, and the *byte* part means one character, so the term means, basically, one thousand characters. Because computers measure everything in powers of twos rather than tens, a kilobyte is actually 1,024 bytes. But you can forget that part; just think of 1KB as 1,000 characters.

5. MB (or just M)

This stands for *Megabyte*, or about one million letters or numbers (characters). This measurement comes into play when people are talking about floppy or hard disk capacities and the amount of installed memory.

6. MHz

This stands for *Megahertz*, a measurement of how fast the computer's microprocessor runs. A *Hertz* is one cycle per second, and since *mega* means *million*, we're talking about one million cycles per second here—a lot. But believe it or not, one million cycles is an appallingly slow speed for a computer. The earliest IBM PC ran at 4.77MHz. Today's systems run at 20MHz or more, with the fastest widely available models running at 66MHz.

7. MS-DOS

The official name for Microsoft's disk operating system (DOS). Most people just shorten this to DOS.

8. RAM

Short for *Random-Access Memory*. This is your computer's internal memory, which you can think of as being like the countertop in

your kitchen. On the countertop, you place the items you're working with at the moment. The stuff you're not using stays down in the drawers and cabinets. In computers, RAM is like the countertop, while the drawers and cabinets are like the hard disk. RAM is measured the same way you measure disk capacity (KB and MB).

9. ROM

Short for *Read-Only Memory*. Every computer has some of this, and it helps the system get started when you turn it on or restart. It's pretty unimportant, and you can forget about it.

10. SVGA

Refers to *Super* VGA. The VGA (Video Graphics Array) video standard has swept the PC world—almost all systems today are sold with VGA video adapters and monitors. Super VGA is an improvement on VGA that offers a sharper screen, more colors, and more detail.

11. TSR

Refers to *Terminate-and-Stay-Resident*, a type of program that isn't actually a very good type to use. When you quit most programs, they leave the memory and go back quietly and harmlessly to your hard disk. TSR programs, however, remain in memory, even if you quit them. The idea is that you can switch to these programs by using a special key combination called a *hot key*.

TSR programs sometimes conflict with each other, or with applications, crashing your computer and wiping out your work. It's best to avoid them.

12. VGA

Short for *Video Graphics Array*. VGA is the standard for today's personal computer video adapters and monitors. If you're using a 386 or 486 computer, chances are good that it has a VGA adapter and monitor. The best systems today, however, come with Super VGA (SVGA) adapters and monitors.

12 Most Common DOS Error Messages

1. Bad command or file name

Cause: DOS can't find a program with that name in the current directory. Perhaps you typed a file name incorrectly. Or maybe it's not in the current directory. Or maybe it just doesn't exist.

Solution: Try typing the command again, checking your spelling carefully. If necessary, change to the directory that contains the file. If you still can't find the file, you might find some additional help in Chapter 20.

2. Duplicate file name or file not found

Cause: You tried to rename a file, but the name is already used. Or you mistyped the file name and DOS couldn't find the file.

Solution: If you typed the name of the file correctly, rename it using a different name. If you misspelled the name of the file, check your spelling and try again.

TIP

> To see whether the file exists in the current directory, type **DIR** followed by the file name (as in **DIR JUNK.DOC**).

3. File cannot be copied onto itself

Cause: You're trying to copy a file, but you messed up typing the destination file name or location.

Solution: Type the **COPY** command again. If you're copying the file to the same directory, you must give the destination file a new name (for example, COPY JUNK.DOC TRASH.DOC). If you're

341

copying the file to a different directory (but with the same name), you have to include path and/or drive information (for example, COPY JUNK.DOC A:).

4. **General failure reading (or writing) Drive *X*. Abort, Retry, Fail?**

Cause: DOS can't access the disk, but it can't figure out why not.

Solution: Relax. Despite the terrifying connotations of "general failure," this probably isn't serious. You've probably just inserted an unformatted disk into the floppy disk drive. Press F to cancel the command. Then type **C:** and press Enter to make drive C current. If you want to format the disk, you can format it now. (Chapter 7 contains the dirt on formatting disks.)

5. **Insufficient disk space**

Cause: At last! A DOS message that's actually understandable. Simply put, you've run out of room on this disk.

Solution: If you're trying to copy something to a floppy disk, re-move the disk and get another one that has more room. If you get this message while using a hard disk, delete unwanted files.

6. **Invalid directory**

Cause: You tried to change to a directory, but something went wrong. There are two possibilities. First, you may have mistyped the directory name, or left out some of those important back-slashes. Second, the directory may not exist—maybe you deleted it or never created it.

Solution: Try typing the command again, and type the full path name, including all those backslashes. If you haven't created the directory or you deleted it, create it again.

I HATE PCs!

TIP

The only time you can leave out the backslashes is when you're changing to a subdirectory of the current directory. For example, suppose you're in C:\DOCS. You can change to C:\DOCS\JUNK by typing **CD JUNK** and pressing Enter. But you can't change from C:\ to C:\WORK\BORING by typing **CD BORING**.

7. Invalid drive specification

Cause: You typed a drive letter in a DOS command, but DOS doesn't think there's any such drive. If you have drives A, B, and C, but refer to a drive D in a command, for example, you get this message.

Solution: Retype the command, using valid drive letters.

8. Invalid file name or file not found

Cause: You tried to rename a file, but you used illegal characters in the new file name.

Solution: Type a new name that uses legal characters (stick to the letters A through Z, and the numbers 0 through 9).

9. Invalid number of parameters, Invalid parameter

Cause: DOS can't understand the command you typed.

Solution: Look up the command again to make sure you're typing it correctly.

10. Non-system disk or disk error

Cause: Stay calm. Don't panic. This problem is minor. A floppy disk was in drive A when you turned on or restarted your computer, and this disk does not contain DOS.

Solution: Remove the disk and press any key to restart the computer.

11. Not ready reading Drive *X*. Abort, Retry, Fail?

Cause: The floppy disk drive doesn't contain a disk, or the drive door is unlatched.

Solution: Put a disk in the drive, latch the door, and press R for Retry.

Checklist

▼ If you get this message when trying to access a hard disk, it's very bad news. Get your local DOS wizard *immediately*, and don't forget to tell the wizard to bring *disk recovery software*.

▼ Don't press F for Fail. If you do, you get the message `Current drive is no longer valid`, which sounds worse than it is. (If this happens, type **C:** and press Enter to make drive C the new current drive.

---

12. Write protect error writing Drive *X*; Abort, Retry, Fail?

Cause: You tried to delete a file on a write-protected disk. Or you tried to copy a file to a write-protected disk.

Solution: If you're using a 3.5-inch disk, turn the disk over, and move the little write-protect tab down so that it covers the hole on the upper left corner of the disk. If you're using a 5.25-inch disk, remove the tape that covers the write-protect notch. Then reinsert the disk and press R to retry the command.

TIP

Before you unprotect a disk, make sure that there isn't a compelling reason to keep the disk protected. One of your coworkers is going to be pretty miffed if you write over the only copy of an important file on a protected disk.

12 Stupid (But Fun) Things to Do with Your Computer

1. **Read palms.**

   PALMISTRY for ALL is a shareware application that graphically covers every conceivable aspect of palmistry, including lines, contours, textures, size, shape, and ring finger choice. You will quickly learn how to read palms and give those "personal comments" that convince your patron that you really are a palm reader and not a computer user craving excitement.

2. **Develop your extra-sensory perception.**

   Guess the target color that the computer selects at random, or try to use your psychokinetic ability to influence the computer as it chooses the color. The key: Development of Mental Energy (DOME), a shareware application. May the Force be with you.

3. **Talk to a therapist.**

   ELIZA, widely available as a non-copyrighted free program, responds to your typed input in ways that elicit further response, such as, "Why does that bother you?" It isn't too hard to figure out the gimmick—the program searches for key words in your typed input, and spits back canned responses. But why should that bother you?

4. **Build a city.**

   You start with virgin territory and begin by providing the basics: power, transport, zoning for industry and commerce. Then the people start moving in. Your challenges as mayor: Raise enough revenue without choking off economic development, Provide

enough jobs without destroying the environment through industrial pollution, Keep crime down without creating a police state. In short, do the impossible. The program: Sim City (Maxis Software).

5. **Apply color vibrations to your daily life.**

According to the author of SPECTRAGEMS, a shareware application, the vibrations of sounds given to you at birth in the form of your name have a unique color spectrum—which means (for some reason that I don't quite get) that certain colors will have a definite effect on your life. You can use your VGA to display just the right colors to get you going. Today, I think nothing short of a rich raspberry will do.

6. **Generate poetry automatically.**

From a database of 15,000 words, POETRY GENERATOR (a shareware application) combines words randomly to generate thousands of original poems, from 4 to 12 lines in length. Most of them are unspeakably stupid, but their very randomness unhinges you from convention and cliché, and conceivably could help you write better poetry.

7. **Let the computer complete words and phrases.**

MINDREADER is the opposite of POETRY GENERATOR—it's a word processing program that draws on a database of word endings to guess what you're trying to type, right down to the last cliché. If MINDREADER can, the program completes the word or phrase for you. Here's how it works: when you've typed a certain number of letters, the word couldn't possibly be anything else, so MINDREADER adds the rest of the letters for you. The more you use it, the better it gets at guessing what you're trying to type.

8. Beat the lottery.

Lots of programs here. Use statistical analysis to predict the most likely combination of big winners. Retire early on your own Caribbean island. Take me with you.

9. Install your own voice mail system.

With BigMouth, a voice mail adapter for 286/386 systems (DemoSource), you can set up your own voice mail system at home. Just imagine! "To speak to Chrissie, press 2 pound now. To speak to Barbie, press 3 pound now. If you are a telephone advertiser, please hold, and enjoy listening to 'Stairway to Heaven' 54 times; one of us will be happy to speak to you then."

10. Design your vegetable garden on-screen.

SPROUT! (Abracadata) automatically snaps your vegetables to the correct row and plant spacing, and lays out a time table based on a database of seven climate regions. Watering the computer is, however, not recommended.

11. Create a model railroad without filling up the basement.

PC-RAILROAD, a shareware application, lets you run up to five model trains on predesigned layouts. Or you can create your own layouts.

12. Analyze handwriting.

HANDWRITING ANALYST, yet another shareware application, lets you analyze anyone's handwriting and produces a detailed report. You examine size, connectedness, expansion, loops, pressure, and many other revealing clues to personality and character.

I HATE PCs!

12 Reasons to Upgrade Your Hardware

1. You need more memory.

I'll bet you're using Microsoft Windows, and you want to use one of those memory-hungry applications that requires 4MB or more of RAM. You can probably solve this problem by adding more memory to your present computer. Generally, computers come with much less memory than the maximum that can be installed. (If you want to know more about memory—and adding memory— flip back to Chapter 6.)

2. You need more speed.

Everyone wants more speed—video speed, math computation speed, disk speed, the works. What kind of speed do you need?

Checklist

▼ If you're running Windows and the screen updates slowly, you can get a huge improvement by adding a video accelerator board to your system. (Chapter 8 uncovers the mysteries of computer video systems.)

▼ If you're working with spreadsheets full of numerical data and the computer takes forever to calculate formulas, you can get improved performance by installing a math coprocessor. (Chapter 5 tells more.)

▼ If your hard disk seems to take forever to access data, you can get improved performance by installing a faster hard disk. (Get a bigger one, while you're at it.)

continues

349

I HATE PCs!

▼ The suggestions listed here work best with 386SX and "higher" systems. (Chapter 5 provides an explanation of these numbers.) If you have a system based on the 8088, 8086, or 80286 processors, you'd probably be better off putting your money into a 486 rather than messing around with upgrading your present system.

▼ If you have a pokey old 386SX running at 16MHz (like mine), don't run out and buy a new, spiffy 486 just yet; you might be able to get a new motherboard for your present computer for a few hundred bucks.

3. You need more disk space.

There's no such thing as enough disk space, as you've probably discovered. That 40MB hard disk that seemed enormous when you bought it turns out to be barely adequate for your applications and data. But before running out and getting a bigger drive, think about running a *disk compression utility*. This utility can double or even triple the amount of storage space on your drive, without posing any risk to your data. (Look at Chapter 17 to learn more.)

TIP

You can add a second hard drive to most modern systems. To get 180MB, then, you can keep your existing 120MB drive and add a relatively inexpensive 60MB drive. In addition, chances are pretty slim that both hard disks would fail at the same time. By keeping valuable files on both drives, you've given yourself an extra margin of data security.

4. **You're sick and tired of the wrong-disk-size shuffle.**

Your computer has one floppy disk drive: a 3.5 incher. And so what size disk does your colleague send you while you're collaborating on a foundation grant proposal? According to Murphy's Law, there is a 3:1 probability that the disk will be a 5.25-inch disk. You'll be in for a hassle to transfer the data to a 3.5-inch disk so that you can use it.

A quick solution: Get a second floppy drive in That Other Size. This is a cheap upgrade, but don't try doing it yourself. Strange things have to be done to hidden switches inside the system unit for this upgrade to succeed.

5. **You want your computer to be able to bark.**

Sound is currently one of the hottest upgrades going. More and more applications are available that can use stereo, digital sound— just imagine what that error beep is going to sound like in stereo! To add sound to your system, you need a sound board and sound software. (Flip to Chapter 11 for a discussion of sound-related hardware.)

6. **You want better print output.**

That old, dot-matrix printout just won't cut it anymore. But if you're using an inkjet or laser printer, chances are you can get better print output by adding *fonts* to your system. This can be done in lots of ways, as Chapter 10 explains. If you're using Windows, though, a good bet is TrueType font technology, which shows up on-screen and automatically prints on most inkjet and laser printers. Package deals advertised everywhere give you 100 TrueType fonts for about a buck a font.

7. **You want color.**

If you're working with a monochrome system, you may be envious—quite rightly—of those folks working with color monitors. Personally, I prefer color because it makes information easier to see on-screen; you don't have to hunt around so much to find that command option name, because it's staring at you in bright red letters.

You can upgrade any PC to a color VGA system. You'll need both a VGA monitor and a VGA adapter card (as explained in Chapter 8). If you're using an 8088 or 8086, get an 8-bit VGA card. If you're using a 286, 386, or 486, get a 16-bit Super VGA card with at least 1MB of video RAM, and try to find a 15-inch monitor rather than the run-of-the-mill 14 inchers. The extra inch actually adds approximately 20 percent more space.

8. **You want a better keyboard.**

This isn't as self-indulgent as you might think. A lot of cheap clone computers come with cheap, mushy-feeling keyboards, which are a drag to use. In fact, they're even dangerous because they increase your chances of developing a repetitive strain injury (RSI). See Chapter 9 for a discussion of keyboards.

9. **You want a mouse.**

People tend to be divided on the merits of mice, and that's okay. Some people just *hate* taking their hands away from the keyboard. But mice are very handy for choosing commands and for editing text. And if you're using Windows, the mouse is practically a necessity—just about every Windows procedure is much easier with a mouse than with the keyboard equivalents. See Chapter 11 for a discussion of mice and their non-rodent brethren.

10. **You want to take advantage of the latest software.**

Today's programs include lots of new, snazzy features, such as TrueType fonts. However, you can't take advantage of some of these programs unless you're using an up-to-date system. For example, Microsoft FoxPro for Windows requires a 386—a 286 won't do. And even if a program *will* run on a 286, you should know that programmers rather cavalierly *assume* that you're using a "reasonably good" computer—which, for them, means a fast 386 or a 486. If you're using an old clunky 386SX-16 like mine, the latest programs run like molasses.

11. **You want to avoid spending $2,000 on an encyclopedia.**

Get a CD-ROM drive instead, and equip it with the New Grolier Electronic Encyclopedia—a 21-volume work with over 33,000 entries. While you're at it, get *U.S. Atlas*, *New York Public Library Desk Reference*, *Dictionary of 20th Century History*, *Webster's New World Dictionary*, *Software Toolworks' World Atlas*, *Countries of the World on CD-ROM*, and please, don't skip the *KBG-CIA World Factbook*. Chances are, you'll outclass your local library's reference section.

12. **You want status.**

Having a "fully loaded 486" is a status symbol in a lot of organizations. But consider this: next year, the status symbol is going to be having a fully loaded Pentium system. (*Pentium* is Intel's all-time-dumb name for the processor that would have been called 586, if it weren't for the fact that other companies can use this number if they want to.) Do you really want to play this game? It's going to be expensive.

I HATE
Index

I HATE PCs!

INDEX

F

F1 (Help) function key, 146
Fastback Plus utility, 273
FAT (file allocation table), 313
fax/modem boards, 187-188
fields (databases), 267
File Manager, 18, 116, 242-244, 255, 259
File menu commands
    Create Directory, 258
    Exit, 67
    Exit Windows, 67
    Rename, 252
    Search, 252
    Select Files, 247
file servers, 190
FileMaker Pro, 268
files, 208
    backups, 272, 332
    configuration files, 30
    copying, 233-236, 249-250, 309-311
    corrupt, 307
    deleting, 229-233, 248, 255-257
    displaying, 244-245, 251
    downloading through modems, 183
    listing, 42-44
    MOUSE.SYS, 307
    moving, 236-237, 250-251
    names, 209
        extensions, 209
        renaming, 237, 251-252
        wild cards, 216-217
    restoring, 273
    saving (troubleshooting), 311
    searching for, 238, 252-254
    selecting, 247
    undeleting, 255-257
    viewing contents, 226
filters, monitors, 332
finances, 271
floppy disks, 107
    backups, 272
    capacity, 109-110
    density, 109-110
    double-sided, 109
    drives, 73, 85, 112-113
    error messages, 313
    files, displaying, 244-245
    formatting, 109, 114-118, 311-312
    inserting, 329
    low-density, 117
    naming, 115
    purchase considerations, 108-112
    reformatting, 311-312
    sectors, 118
    tracks, 118
    unprotecting, 113
    volume label, 115
    write-protected, 113-114
floppy drives, 108
folders, directories, 245-246
fonts, 263, 156-159, 351
FORMAT command (DOS), 116
Format Disk command (Disk menu), 117

I HATE PCs!

I HATE PCs!

I HATE PCs!

INDEX

STATS
Q 320